YOU AND YOUR CAT

YOU AND YOUR CAT
The Ultimate Relationship

VIDA ADAMOLI

Illustrated by Susan Hellard

Piccadilly Press • London

*In memory of Micia, Hollywood and Conker.
And to Frankie, Jessie, Ted, Felix and all the other
feline friends with whom I enjoy a meaningful
relationship – V.A.*

*This book is dedicated in loving memory
to Squirrel – S.H.*

Phototypeset from author's disk
Printed and bound by The Bath Press, Avon
for the publishers, Piccadilly Press Ltd.,
5 Castle Road, London NW1 8PR

A catalogue record for this book is available
from the British Library

ISBN: 1 85340 223 0

Vida Adamoli lives in south east London. Although British she has spent
most of her adult life in Rome where she was a film translator for,
among others, Bertolucci and Felini. She had a woman's afternoon chat
show on Southern Television for many years and she has had a number
of other books published including *Amazing Animals* (Robson Press).
This is her first book for Piccadilly Press.

Susan Hellard lives in North London with her two cats. She is a very
well-known illustrator working in both advertising and publishing. She
has illustrated numerous books, many for Piccadilly Press.

CONTENTS

Introduction

Bibliography

Veni, Vidi, Vici

Introduction – Micia

I was brought up in a family with a strict no-pet rule.
When I was nine, however, I was permitted to keep the
two goldfish I'd won at an Easter fair because the
consensus was that fish didn't really count. I christened
them Goldie and Firefly and kept them in a fruit bowl
with a sprig of plastic seaweed donated by my best
friend. I had them for three glorious days. On the fourth
I returned from a trip to the swimming baths to find
Goldie floating belly up. Firefly followed a few hours
later. I buried them in the garden under the apple tree,
marked the place with a circle of stones and wept
copious tears of grief.

The reason we were not allowed pets was because my
father regarded all animals with distaste. He particularly
disliked cats, and their habit of sinuously rubbing
against legs was something he found positively
repugnant. His ailurophobia had a subconscious effect
on me, for I grew up ignoring cats and focusing my pet-
longing exclusively on dogs. Indeed, at the age of 15 I
defiantly spent all my savings on a black poodle puppy

and threatened to kill myself if I was parted from it. There were several explosive scenes but I got my way.

My involvement with cats started only after I married an Italian and went to live in Rome. Rome is a city of cats. Teeming tribes, fed by devoted 'gattare' on fish heads and pasta, haunt the Forum, the Colosseum, the Theatre of Marcellus and other enclaves of the ancient world. Descended from forebears imported from cat-worshipping Egypt, they bask on toppled columns and chunks of weed-choked stone and marble, observing with haughty detachment the human bustle going on around them. Much as I admired them, however, it wasn't these magnificent strays that ensnared my heart. It was Micia. Micia (Italian for Puss) was a small, lean, idiosyncratic, grey and white tabby. She was born into the large community of feral cats that control the rat population of a tiny coastal village halfway between Rome and Naples. The circumstances in which we got her were dramatic. A gang of local boys – notorious for ill-treating animals – had killed the mother and were disposing of her offspring by bouncing them off a high wall. Word of what they were doing reached the ears of my two small sons, who immediately left their game and rushed to the rescue. By the time they arrived on the scene only one kitten was still alive. Fists flying, they attempted to secure her release commando-style. Defeat, however, was inevitable and swift. While his henchmen held them down, the ringleader picked the survivor up by its slither of a tail and dangled it in their faces. 'You want it?' he said with a mocking grin. 'Then you pay!'

Negotiations were long and drawn-out. Offers were made, rejected, re-presented and rejected again. Eventually the approach of evening – and suppertime – forced them to bring the transaction to a close. Micia's liberation was secured for the pooled resources of my sons' pockets: 90 lire, a safety pin and a tangle of multi-coloured elastic bands.

The battle-scarred deliverers carried her home wrapped in a T-shirt; a trembling, pathetic, newly-fledged life entity barely the size of a fist. One look at the orphaned scrap and there was no question but that she would stay. The spaghetti was forgotten as we all took turns in feeding her warm milk with a teaspoon, after which the kitten was scooped up by my pregnant sister and tucked snugly into the big front pocket of her maternity smock (where like a baby kangaroo – or furry foetus – she spent the rest of that summer).

In due course Micia expressed approval at her comfortable new surroundings with a low, rasping purr. Having no previous experience of cats and never having heard the sound before, both boys were terrified. 'We have to get her to the vet!' the eldest exclaimed in anguish. 'She's dying of asthma!'

But despite the odd purr Micia showed remarkably little gratitude at being rescued from her fate. She quickly developed a nagging whine and generally behaved in a way indicative of the autocratic, bad-tempered creature she was to become. The response of each member of the family to this strong-willed feline was different. My husband considered her an unwelcome disruption and she returned the sentiment by regularly defecating under his – and only his – dining room chair. My sons were her devoted slaves and she treated them as such. For myself, I refused to be dictated to and we embarked on a battle of wills that was to keep us occupied for 18 long years.

Micia's most lethal weapon was her vocal cords. She was capable of a hectoring yowl that grew in ear-splitting crescendo until I was beaten into submission and she achieved her objective. This tactic was used in winter to get the central heating turned on during the scheduled off hours (no hot water bottle, thank you, she insisted on lying on the top of one particular radiator). It was also used as a dinner bell and to communicate any negative opinions about food.

Micia was one of life's finicky eaters and what was acceptable one day was not necessarily so the day after. A bowl of something she deemed unappetizing would trigger a verbal remonstration that could go on for hours. On one occasion she went on a yowling, three-day hunger strike until I capitulated and threw away the tin of perfectly good chicken and gave her the rabbit she wanted instead.

What I found most difficult, however, were those occasions when Micia decided to share my bed. Had she been content to curl quietly at my feet this would have been acceptable, but that was not her style. Having from kittenhood slept with one or other of the boys (who called her 'La Principessa di Casa' – Princess of the

House – and were prepared to do anything for her comfort), she insisted on wrapping herself around my neck like a fur boa. And as if that wasn't bad enough, she kept her whiskery nose pressed against mine because she liked the feel of warm breath blowing in her face. To maintain this nose-to-nose contact she spent half the night tramping back and forth over my head. I tried, of course, locking her out of the bedroom but even ear-plugs were no match for her outrage.

Micia was with us for 18 years, dying two years after we returned to live in England. Although she missed the sunshine and large terrace of our Rome flat, it was old age not homesickness that killed her. The loss of my Best Enemy and Dearest Sparring Partner left a void that hasn't been filled. Indeed, my eyes still brim with nostalgic tears when the sudden sound of screeching brakes evokes the memory of her strident commands. It's on occasions such as these that I find myself pondering the nature of feline-human relationships. What are they and what makes them special? And what was it about an undersized, unprepossessing feline that so captured my affections that I allowed her to disturb my work, my sleep, my social life and – let's face it – generally push me around?

Chapter 1

PETS AND PEOPLE –
THE EMOTIONAL BOND

ME OR IT

Peter is a 36-year-old freelance book illustrator and the divorced father of two little girls. Eight months after his divorce became final he started going out with Carole, also an artist. As a couple they were well-suited. Apart from a shared passion for opera, both were active environmentalists and both understood the committed nature of the other's work. But, as Shakespeare said, the course of true love never did run smooth. And in Peter and Carole's case the problem reared up in the shape of a large ginger tom called Gus.

Gus had been with Peter for three years, ever since he moved out of the family home into the garden flat he now occupied. It was a painful adjustment, but without Gus's demonstratively loving companionship Peter would have found it much worse. Unfortunately, however, Carole could not stand him. She particularly objected to Gus sharing their bed and insisted he was banished. Peter refused. After all, he pointed out, it wasn't as though she was allergic or anything, nor could she say that Gus (who only settled himself at the bottom of Peter's side of the bed) ever disturbed them. Eventually Carole told him he would have to choose between them. It was a hard decision but in the end Peter chose Gus.

PERFECT COMPANIONS HAVE FOUR FEET

All relationships are, to a certain extent, mysterious. Much of what attracts or repels us is instinctual and hard to explain. It is usually that indefinable something – a certain look, way of moving, energy, aura – that draws us like a magnet. Indeed, it is when choosing a mate that rationality and logic are most conspicuously absent. At heart, most people yearn for the perfect relationship, an almost mystical rapport in which the physical, mental, spiritual and emotional are expressed in total harmony. Rarely achieved in human interaction, there are those who say the nearest they get to it is with their pets. As Collette (whose turbulent life taught her a thing or two) wrote, 'Our perfect companions never have fewer than four feet.' Some people would go further and state, 'The perfect companion is nothing other than The Cat!'

It has to be said that *Felis catus*, first domesticated between 3500 and 4500 years ago, has always elicited extremes of response from the human species. During the long years of our communal history The Cat has been deity and demon, friend and foe, protected by emperors and viciously hunted to near extinction. In my own life, I have met people who recoil from it in fear, people who sneeze and break out in rashes the moment they're in its presence, and people who condemn it as cruel, devious, sly, scheming and a consummate thief. I've also met those who say it's not that they dislike cats exactly, but that something about their eyes/walk/ spring/purr/tail etc gives them a feeling of strange, skin-prickling unease.

It is true to say that a cat does not give unconditional love in the great slobbery, tail-thwacking, dollops a dog does. The dog is described as devoted and loyal, the cat self-possessed and independent. Certainly a cat is never subservient and its friendship is harder won - it will be your companion but never your slave.

THE CASE FOR CATS

In my experience, the world can be neatly divided into Cat People and Dog People – Us and Them. Cat People say Dog People are basically insecure types who demand unquestioning obedience from their pets and the constant reassurance of being in physical and emotional control. (They will tell you that Adolf Hitler, Napoleon, Alexander the Great and the lantern-jawed, whip-cracking PE teacher at their primary school were all notable cat-haters.) Cat People, they claim, are the opposite; a sensitive, creative, thoughtful bunch who regard the feline gracing their home as a respected and self-sufficient equal. (At this point a roll-call of ailurophile writers, painters, musicians, actors, prime ministers and august statesmen is trotted out.)

Even without being besottedly rapturous, however, anyone whose affections have been engaged by a cat knows it has a lot going for it in the pet stakes. It is clean, graceful, sleekly muscular, silky soft to touch, undeniably beautiful and tailor-made for the human lap. Although it does not bestow its regard lightly, once it does, you have a friend for life. It will keep you company while you work (Micia insisted on sprawling across my desk and swatting the paper waving in the typewriter), doze on your knee while you watch TV – even go to the loo with you if you let it. It will also offer its warm, purring comfort on those nights when life is tough and nobody else seems to either understand or care. As Bruce Fogel says about pets in his book *Pets and Their People*, cats satisfy our need for 'warm furries'.

THE FELINE MYSTERY BIT

But even the most cosy, indulged and well-fed cat is only partially tamed. Its feral ancestry exerts a strong influence and the wild animal still lurks in its heart.

In his book *Her Majesty the Cat*, Fernand Mery says that God made the cat in order that man might have the pleasure of caressing a tiger. Anybody who has observed the muscles rippling down its back as it runs, the power of its effortless spring, the murderous sharpness of its pointed teeth and unsheathed claws, the fire-flame flash as its eyes ignite the dark, will understand immediately what he means. To watch it stalk a shadow, freeze in preparation for ambush, explode in hissing, spitting rage, is to understand that its inherent nature is beast of prey. Indeed, for many people it is the awareness of the cat's feline otherness, its aspect of alien mystery, that adds special significance to their relationship with it.

FULFILLING YOUR COMPLEX YEARNINGS

Human beings have been giving houseroom to cats for many thousands of years. The fact that this cross-species arrangement is so enduring is testimony to the obvious satisfaction it gives both parties. Certainly the cat's role as rat catcher, mouse exterminator and snake killer was what first earned it a place at the hearth. Nowadays, however, the average pet is there to fulfil the more complex yearnings of the human psyche rather than chase rodents.

People, of course, differ enormously, as do their needs and desires. It stands to reason, therefore, that each person's relationship with his or her cat will reflect that.

Leonard, whose cats, Pye and Tosca, are the reigning monarchs of his garden flat, talked of the privilege he felt when either deigned to fall asleep on his knee. 'Like all hunters, cats are by nature wary and suspicious,' he explained. 'When they use me as a bed they're showing how much they trust me. I consider that trust the greatest compliment.'

Julian expressed similar sentiments when talking about his magnificent, panther-black tom Frankie (who comes rushing out of nowhere the moment he hears, amid all the other traffic noises, the sound of Julian's 750cc Kawasaki). 'I admire Frankie and I envy him,' he said. 'He's strong, intelligent, brave, resourceful, free-spirited – and the local Romeo to boot. He's a prince among creatures and I'm honoured he accepts my hospitality and lets me share his life.'

Of course, the fact that pets can't talk (or answer back!) is part of their charm and allows us to endow them with qualities of our choice. Courage, compassion, artfulness, creativity – we see what we want or need to see. Go into any cat-lover's home and you will find philosophers, adventurers, aristocrats, psychics, thieves, cowards, courtesans and fraudsters ruling the roost. One of my neighbours in Rome had a large brindled tabby called Ingmar who spent most of his day sitting among the pots of geraniums that crowded her small terrace. Compared to the feline harridan I lived with, he always struck me as a contented, well-adjusted and contemplative sort. My neighbour, however, insisted otherwise. 'I called him Ingmar because, although he was born in the shadow of St Peter's, he suffers from the Scandinavian Gloom. Even as a kitten you could see he was a depressive.'

But introvert or extrovert, valiant or craven, there are certain things about our animals on which all cat-lovers agree. Their beauty and grace is unrivalled and to stroke the sleek, luxuriant fur of a compact, muscular, lap-sized body is both physically sensual and emotionally profound. Charles Baudelaire, the 19th-century French poet, put it nicely when he said:

Come, lovely cat, and rest upon my heart,
And let my gaze dive in the cold
Live pools of thine enchanted eyes that dart
Metallic rays of green and gold.

My fascinated hands caress at leisure
Thy head and supple back, and when
Thy soft, electric body fills with pleasure
My thrilled and drunken fingers, then

Thou changest to my woman; for her glance,
Like thine, most lovable of creatures,
Is icy deep, and cleaving as a lance.

Chapter 2

AND WHAT A PERSONALITY

All right, so we're guilty of projecting a lot on to Puss that maybe isn't there. Nevertheless, it is also true that each cat is an individual and as such, each has a distinctive character just as we do. Indeed, your ultimate relationship will depend on understanding your cat's personality. Human beings can improve and undergo radical change, cats can't and won't. You need to accept your feline's personality and be prepared to accommodate it. There are definite types that every cat lover will certainly recognise. They are:

THE PERPETUAL KITTEN

The Perpetual Kitten is the feline Peter Pan, the Moggie Who Won't Grow Up. At an age when other cats have to be coaxed, it is still frisking around with as much

9

delight and enthusiasm as ever. I know a 10-year-old
Burmese called Smokey who spends much of his day
diving into paper bags, demolishing newspapers,
pouncing on passing ankles and chasing anything that
rustles when it moves. His special toys are a squeaky
rubber mouse and a table-tennis ball which, being light,
responds most satisfactorily to a swat from his paw.
Most healthy adult cats, however, enjoy a game or two
with their humans. But as the 16th-century French
essayist Michel de Montaigne wrote, 'When I play with
my cat, who knows whether I make her more sport than
she makes me?'

THE LAP CAT

Lap Cats are the princes and princesses of the feline
world. Phenomenally lazy, they limit their activities to
yawning, stretching, grooming and making themselves
comfortable. Spoilt, petted, indulged and adored, they

do what they want, when they want and how they want. They like big squishy cushions, long stroking sessions, and are perfectly happy to be carried around instead of having to walk. The true Lap Cat is the result of years of relentless spoiling and the death of an adoring owner can change their circumstances overnight. Mary Rossi, who died in 1986, was aware of this problem. She left Minky, her twelve-year-old Lap Cat, £10,000 to keep her in style for the rest of her life. The guardians of this privileged animal were expected to provide a menu which included poached cod in parsley sauce, boiled chicken with a side portion of chopped livers, and her favourite brand of tinned tuna.

THE THIEF

The majority of feline pilferers are neither hungry nor homeless, they simply have a thieving heart. Sally, my friend Geraldine's extremely well-looked-after black and white puss, regularly appears over the garden fence with a purloined sausage, piece of pie or even biscuit in her mouth. On one occasion she actually had a whole fish clamped tightly in her jaws. Half-cooked and practically sizzling, it was clear Sally had actually nicked someone's lunch straight out of the frying pan. Geraldine has tried scolding and confiscating her animal's ill-gotten gains. So far, however, neither tactic has shown any effect. Sally continues shamelessly offending.

THE HUNTER

There's a riddle that goes: How do you spell mousetrap in three letters? Answer: C A T. And it's true; by nature all cats are carnivorous hunters and much of a kitten's play is to prepare it for that role. Nevertheless, most people would agree that one of the least pleasurable aspects of cohabiting with a feline is waking up to find a furry or feathered offering tucked under the bed, inside a slipper, or even gasping its last, inches from your face.

In some cats the hunting instinct is much more powerful than in others. Towser, who died in 1987, was considered one of the greatest mousers of all times. Her territory was the Glenturret distillery near Crieff, Tayside, where it is said she accounted for the deaths of a staggering 28,000 mice. Six-year-old Tosca, whose

Cricklewood garden backs onto a railway line, has been a ferocious hunter since kittenhood. On 10 July 1992, she presented her squeamish, vegan human with five mice, two birds and a grass snake – all laid out in a row on the bottom of his duvet. Neutered females are the most likely to bring back live animals. This is said to be a response to their frustrated maternal urges.

THE NEUROTIC

Neurotic cats, like neurotic people, exhibit a range of personality and behavioural disorders. For example, a cat who spends most of its time indoors deprived of stimulus from the natural environment will release pent-up energy in those mad, senseless dashes that can make an observer think the animal has seen a ghost or is having a seizure. (Mind you, cats also do this when they are feeling full of beans.) Other neurotic manifestations are fouling the house – often caused by the emotional stress of a new rival or moving home – and wool sucking. This last habit is most common among cats who, like Micia, were orphaned or deprived of the nipple too early. Constant yowling, jumping three feet in the air and hiding whenever there is a strange noise or a visitor arrives are other neurotic symptoms.

A tortoiseshell cat belonging to a Derbyshire farmer's wife climbed a 15-foot tree to give birth to three kittens in an abandoned magpie's nest, which seems to me, at least, a singularly neurotic thing to do.

THE GREEDY GUTS

A lot of people believe that left to choose, a cat will naturally opt for the balanced diet that is best for it. Despite being fastidious eaters, however, this is frequently not true. Micia had a passion for butter, gorgonzola rinds and pasta with garlicky sauce. My neighbour's cat, Ingmar, became frenzied with excitement any time there was a sugared doughnut around. In order to get what it wants the Greedy Guts will turn to crime. G. Harding of Islington owned two exceptionally voracious Siamese called Dandelion and Burdock. Although both were able to open cupboards, fridges and any packaging known to man, it was Burdock who was the true master of his art. On one memorable occasion he unzipped a leather flight bag, burrowed through tightly-packed clothing, gnawed his way through three carrier bags and ate a quarter-kilo of extremely hard German sausage – all in under ten minutes. Over-eating carries the same penalty for felines as it does for us: they get fat and the heart and joints suffer. A famous heavyweight Greedy Guts was a tabby called Joseph. He ate his way to a record forty-eight pounds.

THE MATRIARCH

The Matriarch is Top Cat. She dominates the house and its inhabitants – both human and feline – with an autocratic paw. The Matriarch uses mothering behaviour as a controlling device, to both retain and reinforce her dominance. When grooming grown-up kittens, for example, she will continue to hold them down exactly as she did when they were little. A Matriarch will invariably choose the highest perch in a room (chest of drawers, back of chair, top of shutters etc) in order to keep a stern eye on what's going on.

While the other cats might be prepared to eat out of the same dish, not so the Matriarch. Either dinner is served in her own bowl or she won't eat at all. She decides when it's time to sleep and when it's time to play. Indeed, what the other cats in the family do or don't do depends to a large extent on her mood.

Peaseblossom, mother of Sage, Parsley, Rosemary and Thyme, was just such a cat. Her owner, Yvonne, was never under any illusion that it was she who lived in Peaseblossom's house and not the other way round. Yvonne, like the kittens, was also regularly groomed. During these sessions, Peaseblossom would press a restraining paw on the crown of Yvonne's head while she vigorously licked her eyebrows.

THE FUSS POT

All cats are naturally fastidious and know what they like. The Fuss Pot, however, has developed choosiness almost to a fine art. A Fuss Pot insists on everything in its life being exactly as it wants it. Indeed, many an owner has been forced to trawl the shelves of the nearest midnight shop because Tiddles's favourite brand of cat food has run out and she won't accept a substitute. Occasionally, such fussiness can bring unexpected results. In 1983 Mrs Christine Cowton purchased four tins of unlabelled cat food from her local market on the assurance they contained 100 per cent top quality rabbit meat – the only meat her particular Fuss Pot, Snowy, would eat. When she served it up that evening, however, the cat took one mouthful and turned away in disgust. Mrs Cowton opened the next tin, then the third and the fourth, but Snowy turned up her nose disdainfully at them all. To Mrs

Cowton there was only one explanation – the contents were not what they purported to be. She called in consumer protection officials who confirmed that they contained second quality beef! The crooked trader landed a £450 fine and learnt not to underestimate his feline customers again.

THE WIMPY TOM

My sister's cat, Conker, was the archetypal Wimpy Tom. He was small and grey and people would say 'Isn't she lovely!', not realising he was male. She adopted him as a traumatised kitten and watched helplessly as he grew up frightened of everything: other cats, a heavy tread and, most particularly, brooms. This was illustrated to most effect the day she began sweeping under her bed not knowing he was there. Screaming in terror, he burst from under the coverlet and on finding his escape route (the door) closed, actually scrambled halfway up the wall. On another occasion she arrived home to be welcomed by a great commotion coming from the patio garden. She hurried out to find Conker cowering in a corner being dive-bombed by two shrieking blackbirds. Clearly they had found a fledgling missing from the nest and he was being held responsible.

Poor Conker was also the victim of feline bullying. Groups of three or four toms regularly gathered outside his gate to let him know that if he was too wimpy to defend his territory, then he couldn't call it his own. His

worst tormentor was a burly thug called Sooty. Sooty
not only squatted on Conker's window sill, but regularly
slipped into the house to steal his food, too.
Fortunately, however, Conker eventually found an ally
in Puss, the supremely placid old cat who lived next
door. Every day they would spend companionable hours
sitting in her bathtub, after which she would lead the
way into the kitchen where Conker was graciously
invited to share in her dinner.

THE GREAT COMMUNICATOR (SCREAM, SCREAM, SCREAM!)

Anyone who has lived with a Great Communicator
knows they are highly intelligent and that conversation
is an important part of their daily life. Owners soon
become familiar with their feline's vocabulary (the
largest of any animal except *Homo sapiens*), although
it's true to say cats learn to understand our language far
better than we ever do theirs. In my case it was Micia's
'I demand your immediate attention' miaow and her
long, yodelling yowls of complaint that I most
recognised. There were also companionable interludes,
however, when we'd chat away while she watched me
getting on with some chore or other in the kitchen. On
those occasions Micia expressed herself with purrs,
mews and little chirps, gazing up at me with an
expression of polite attention when I replied.

Siamese, of course, are the most famously talkative of

all breeds. They produce sounds ranging from a low purr to a sharp harsh cry and all manner of hisses, growls, puffs and huffs in between.

THE NOSEY PARKER

The Nosey Parker is a close relative of the Perpetual Kitten. In fact, Perpetual Kittens are often Nosey Parkers and vice versa. Insatiably curious, the Nosey Parker can't keep its whiskers out of anything – with forbidden places like the airing cupboard, desk drawer and sewing box having most appeal. Everything new has to be thoroughly inspected, especially any parcel or bulging carrier bag that is brought home. A Nosey Parker's life, however, can be quite hazardous. In 1980, young Bozley decided to explore the family's automatic front loader.

She went through a programme of warm pre-wash, spin and hot wash before her owner became aware of a strange bumping sound and decided to investigate. Rushed to the vet, Bozley was given an injection and eight hours later was fully recovered.

A few years later, a stray cat in the Dutch town of Raalte crawled through a hole in a taxi's chassis and got stuck inside. The unsuspecting cabbie spent the whole day driving around before the stowaway was discovered. It was so wedged that a mechanic had to dismantle the fuel tank before it could be set free. As the taxi driver said, curiosity had almost killed a cat that day.

THE ALLEY CAT

From the age of six weeks, Ambrose had lived with a bank manager, his book-keeper wife and their two school-age children in a three-storey Georgian house in London's Islington district. He was well-fed, well-loved and his comfortable basket occupied the warmest position by the Aga in the kitchen. Despite such favourable circumstances, however, all Ambrose yearned for was life on the street. To his family's despair (and not little embarrassment), he far preferred rifling noisily through stinking dustbins than eating the clean, nourishing meat chunks put on his plate. He prowled the neighbourhood rolling in dirt, getting into fights and hanging out with only the roughest and toughest on the street.

The Alley Cat's heart is the heart of the tramp. He is an anti-conformist, anti-establishment rebel with a string of bad habits as long as his leg. He spurns the quiet, respectable life for the adventure of gutters, rooftops, rubbish dumps and back walls. And as anyone who owns one knows, it's not that the Alley Cat can't learn good manners – simply that he won't.

9 out of 10 cats prefer it.

Chapter 3

YOUR CAT AND YOU
Understanding and Improving Your
Relationship Through Communication

Good communication is the key to all harmonious and rewarding relationships, be they feline or human. To achieve this there must be a two-way interaction in which both parties can express feelings and requirements and trust they'll be understood. Perfect understanding, of course, is a romantic utopia rarely achieved in any relationship, however ideal. However hard we try there will always be occasions when a situation or intention is misread or misconstrued.

Like all relationships, the relationship we make with our cat is largely determined by the love and effort we put into it. We need to remember the cat is a strong individualist, with its own opinions on what it wants for its comfort and wellbeing.

Human beings communicate primarily with spoken language. We also rely on a series of expressive noises, facial expressions, hand gestures and body language. Although the feline vocabulary is limited (as is the vocabulary of all solitary species), the cat nevertheless has a whole repertoire of sounds at its disposal. In order to learn what these sounds mean, we should study our cat as carefully and attentively as it does us.

TALKING

A cat employs a range of sounds to express its needs and emotional states. These include murmurs, trills, hisses, spits, growls, yowls, fully-fledged miaows and, of course, the delightful purr. Depending on the volume and inflexion of tone, we usually know whether Puss is making a polite request, being commanding, lodging an outraged complaint, or simply in the mood for some friendly conversation. Every cat develops its own personal style of expression, but there are certain 'miaow messages' common to all.

1) The first, and for many the most familiar, is the loud, assertive miaow of a feline demanding its owner's immediate attention. Then there is the aggrieved wail informing us that the food/weather/temperature of central heating radiator etc is not what is wanted at all.

2) On a more endearing note there is the soft, chirruping trill with which cats express their pleasure when a loved human comes home.

3) A deeper, throatier yowl indicates fear.

4) And there is no mistaking the screech of a cat that has been hurt or is in pain.

For their part, cats can interpret our tone and grasp the underlying meaning of much of what we say. While not understanding the exact words, they immediately distinguish between affectionate, encouraging remarks and those that are cross and irritable. They respond with pleasure to the sound of their owner's voice, and regular verbal communication is an important part of creating and maintaining this bond. Singing, however, particularly in the alto range, is not always acceptable. Indeed, many cats howl in dismay every time their owner attempts to burst into song. Ginger, a famous feline despot, would actually leap up and smack his mistress in the face on those occasions she forgot herself and started to yodel.

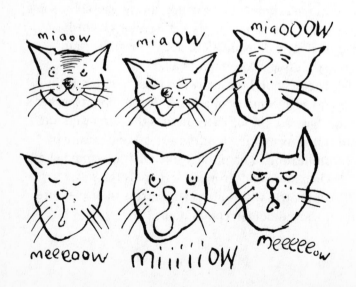

BODY LANGUAGE: FELINE SIGNALS

Feline body language incorporates ear and tail positions, facial expressions, the bristling of fur and posture. Once again, careful observation is the key to learning the messages these various displays convey. In a normal state of lively awareness the ears are perky and upright. Pressed down and back, however, Puss is either frightened – perhaps anticipating a reprimand for misbehaviour – or aggressive and preparing for attack. Ears pricked sharply forward indicate she has focused on something that is commanding her intense interest.

Tails are extremely eleoquent, too. A tail swishing violently from side to side signals anger or anticipation (ie bird watching) lowered and fluffed out – fear; erect and fluffed out – aggression; while erect with a quivering tip is an indication of excitement. Tail twitches can mean irritation or anticipation. They can also signify confusion arising from something their owner has done or is about to do. Greeting a human friend, the cat's tail is held straight up and stiff as a poker. A cowed, frightened or defeated cat, however, slinks its tail between its legs. An alarmed cat drops its tail and hind legs, pricks its ears and looks tense and wary. Happy and attentive, it wanders about waving its tail gently to and fro.

The whiskers of an excited cat bristle out. Frequent blinking and lip licking means it is relaxed. Rolling over and exposing its vulnerable underside is a display of trust as well as an invitation to indulge in a little social interaction. If frightened, however, a cat dilates its eyes and presses its body close to the ground for protection. And when attacked it will make itself look more intimidating by arching its back, bushing out its tail, and erecting the hairs along the length of its back.

TOUCHING

Touch, of course, is another aspect of feline/human dialogue. Indeed, stroking is just about the most pleasurable form of communication for both cat and human alike. Due to the presence of numerous tactile pads known as 'touch spots', a cat's entire body is highly responsive to touch. Touch is central to the feline language of love. We all know the 'nose kiss', the purring 'head nuzzle' into an open, stroking palm, and the sensual 'leg-rub' greeting.

PAW POINTS

There are also cats who use their paws to make a point. My friend Alison's tom, Baxter, has a habit of tapping her smartly on the ankle or knee when she's on the phone, for example, and he wants her attention. Others soon master the art of leaping up to rap on doors or windows if there's no cat flap and they want to be let in.

PHYSICAL CONTACT: SHOWING EACH OTHER AFFECTION

The writer Edgar Allan Poe had a cat called Catalina who would perch on his shoulder for hours when he wrote. Pope Leo XII (1760-1829) had a big greyish-red cat who snoozed happily on his knee (hidden by the papal robes) while he gave audiences. On the other hand, my mother's sleekly independent, tigerish tabby submits to petting with sufferance. And when she does, you know full well you are being graciously humoured and that five minutes is the very most she'll concede you.

Cats don't like smothering; they give affection on their own terms. Indeed, as every cat person knows, physical contact – how much and how often – always depends on the humour of the cat. We've all experienced subjecting our feline to a devoted stroking, scratching, hugging, crooning love-session only to be rewarded by a bored yawn as it slips from our grasp, jumps down, and strolls casually away. Or conversely, those days when it dogs our footsteps determined to occupy our lap each time we sit down. On one occasion I was chatting to my Rome neighbour in the doorway of her flat when Ingmar arrived and plonked himself down on one of her slippered feet. He was having a 'needy' day, she explained, and consequently wouldn't leave her alone. He had even tried wrapping his front paws around her ankle to stop her from walking around.

SLEEPING WITH YOUR MOGGIE

Physical contact is an essential constituent of the emotional bond we form with our feline friend. Touching and stroking create intimacy, and intimacy gives us the closeness, familiarity and warmth which is so important. When the well-known veterinary surgeon, Bruce Fogel, conducted a survey in his practice he found that 50 per cent of cats slept in their owner's bedroom, with 35 per cent actually sharing the bed. Peaseblossom's relationship with her mistress, Yvonne, was such that they shared not only the same bed but the same pillow. This arrangement was discontinued, however, after the night Yvonne awoke to find

Peaseblossom vomiting copiously into her thick, curly black hair.

Arthur and Kate have three magnificent Abyssinians on whom they lavish much affection. Adored though they are, however, the cats are banned from their bedroom. 'Because we love them and share our home with them, it doesn't mean there aren't boundaries,' they say. 'And the bedroom is definitely our space and not theirs.'

THE ART OF PLAYING

A playful cat has irresistible appeal. Certainly one of the great pleasures of sharing one's home with a cat is playing with it or watching it at play. Back in the second century AD, the dignified Roman historian Lucius Coelius was not ashamed to record that his favourite leisure time pursuit was a little frolic with his cat. The great 17th-century naturalist, Edward Topsel, would certainly have understood, as the following passage he wrote on feline play shows: 'Therefore how she beggeth, playeth, leapeth, looketh, catcheth, tosseth with her foot, riseth up to strings held over her head, sometimes creeping, sometimes lying on the back, playing with one foot, sometimes on the belly, snatching now with mouth, and anon with the foot ... '

And Lady Sydney Morgan (1783-1859) had this to say: 'The playful kitten, with its pretty little tigerish gambols, is infinitely more amusing than half the people one is obliged to live with in the world.'

PLAYING TOGETHER

Kittenhood, of course, is when felines are at their most playful. At about three weeks they start rough-and-tumble play-fighting with their litter mates. They ambush each other, roll over on their backs, grapple and generally have great fun. By the time they are a month old the play-fighting has become more elaborate, with chasing, pouncing, clasping with the front legs and kicking energetically with the back ones. As the weeks go by, further play-themes are added. These involve hiding, crouching, pouncing, creeping and swatting – all skills essential to the hunters they will grow up to become.

A kitten needs no coaxing to play. The world is new

and wonderful and made for exploration. Any small moving object is enough to set it off. It chases after falling leaves, pounces on dappled spots of sunlight, ambushes slippered feet, scrambles up table legs and swings from curtains like a circus acrobat. While there are all sorts of special cat toys on the market, more often than not they are hard and heavy and not worth the expense. The ideal play object is light enough to be batted effortlessly across a room and soft enough for feline claws and teeth to grasp it securely. A screwed-up piece of cellophane, for example, a piece of string or the traditional ball of wool, all fit the bill perfectly.

With the right sort of encouragement, a mature cat can retain a playful disposition for most of its life. And for adult humans, especially those without children, a romp with Puss allows them to relive something of their own childhood. Playing with a pet is non-competitive and nobody's out to be the winner. It's fun for fun's sake and provides totally stress-free relaxation. As a cat grows older it develops its own repertoire of favourite games. Through repetition they become treasured rituals and give a sense of specialness to the relationship which that particular feline and human have formed.

VARIATIONS ON GAMES

Variations on cat games are endless. Micia, for example, liked burrowing under the duvet while I made scratching noises with my nails on the cotton cover above her head. Frankie, Julian's panther-like tom, plays an enthusiastic 'fetch' with a scrunched-up Marlboro packet. He retrieves it from the back of whatever piece of furniture it has fallen behind, bounds back to drop it into Julian's outstretched palm, then grins triumphantly while waiting for it to be thrown again. Another cat of my acquaintance dive-bombs her mistress's wastepaper basket for the pleasure of chasing the screwed-up balls of paper that spill out. The heart of all these games, of course, is the interaction they provide. As Esther, a busy GP, says, 'For ten minutes or so before supper, Horlicks and I forget about everything and play with her old blue ball and squeaky rubber mouse. It's our time, just her and me. We both look forward to it and neither of us would miss it for anything.'

MALE OR FEMALE – DOES IT MATTER?

Official opinion is that cats show little difference in temperament once they have been neutered. However, those people I know living with a moggie of each sex seem to disagree. Felix might be soppily affectionate, they declare, but that doesn't mean he isn't all boy with it. And as for Fifi – well, just look at her and you can see she's female through and through.

 Neutering is generally considered the most convenient method of contraception, unless the intention is to breed. Furthermore, neutering has the added advantage of stopping a tom cat spraying and getting involved in bloody fights. But for those people who are morally opposed to de-sexing their animals, alternative methods do exist. A vasectomy for the male and tying the female's fallopian tubes leaves feline sexuality intact without adding to the problem of unwanted kittens. For the female there is also oral contraception.

WHO'S BOSS – CAN PUSS BE TRAINED?

A dog can be trained to dance on its hind legs, leap through flaming hoops, and whizz round a circus ring on the back of a cantering horse. At home it learns to respond to verbal commands and comport itself with the obedience demanded of it by society. A cat, on the other hand, learns only that which it chooses to learn – like opening the fridge or cupboard door to get at food, for example – and will never perform at the command of an owner. Cats are creatures of habit and do not take kindly to their routine being disturbed – particularly where meal times are concerned. If Puss is used to being fed at seven, she will probably start reminding you of the fact 15 minutes earlier. And when your cat fixes you with imploring eyes and a beguilingly-tilted head, it could be that he's not 'asking' for a piece of that succulent salmon, but 'demanding' what he thinks is rightfully his.

Despite the cat's independence, however, bad conduct can be modified in the time-honoured way of rewarding good behaviour and punishing bad. Roger Mugford, the animal psychologist, says combining an angry 'No!' with a swat of a newspaper or squirt from a water-pistol usually gets the message across. Consistency is vital in this re-educating regime, as is catching the offender in the act. (Micia had various unacceptable habits but she was wily enough not to indulge them if there was a witness around.) Cat experts say, however, that the cat regards its human as a larger cat. This should make you the dominant one in the household. Some cats are undoubtedly more forceful and determined than others. Ultimately, however, if your cat is ruling the roost, it's because you are letting it.

Chapter 4

THE MYSTERIES OF CAT POWER

'Ah! cats are a mysterious kind of folk. There is more passing their minds than we are aware of. It comes no doubt from their being so familiar with warlocks and witches.'

Sir Walter Scott (1771-1832) to Washington Irving

The Egyptians loved their cats and venerated them as deities. In China, the souls of Buddhists were believed to reside in cats before passing on to eternal nirvana. In the Middle Ages, Europeans feared them as witches' familiars and allies of the devil. Throughout history the cat has been a symbol of mystery and secret power. The cat belongs to both our familiar daytime world of domesticity and the forbidden, shadowy world of night. It represents an enigmatic link between that which we know and all that we still don't understand.

Most cat people will agree that there often seems to

be something almost telepathic in the harmonious relationship between human and cat. In fact, this undercurrent of communication – termed by some psychologists an 'inner connection' – is so commonplace that many people simply take it for granted. Every now and then, however, situations and circumstances arise in which these mysterious feline abilities are manifest in ways that reason cannot explain. And research seems to show that foremost among these circumstances are negative changes in the physical or emotional wellbeing of a human friend.

A FRIEND IN NEED

Emma fell in love with Steven at first sight. She was a 32-year-old fabric designer and her romantic wedding was the happiest day of her life. As he slipped the ring on her finger, Emma contemplated a future of babies and jam-making and happiness ever after.
Unfortunately, however, it was not to be. Steven soon revealed himself to be a selfish, neglectful husband who was broodingly resentful of her professional success. He did everything he could to undermine her self-confidence and three years later left her for one of her friends.

Emma, who had tried everything to retain his interest and save their marriage, was devastated. She became clinically depressed, unable to eat, sleep, or function normally. For days after Steven's departure she lay in bed, curled in a foetal ball, weeping. Her family lived a five-hour drive away and she couldn't face seeing or speaking to friends. She was alone but for the company of her two Seal Pointed Siamese.

At that time Saki and Lilly were just over a year old. Affectionate and playful though they were, they were also independent creatures who preferred to spend most of each day exploring the world outside. From the onset of Emma's emotional crisis, however, they never left her. Like vigilant book-ends they took up position either side of her, licking her hair, her face, and mewing softly to remind her when it was time for her to prepare their food. Saki and Lilly's needs were the only reality that somehow managed to penetrate the dense layers of her terrible grief and despair.

Emma's recollection of that time remains hazy but she believes she was in bed for over a week. When she eventually got up, weak and dizzy, the cats followed her everywhere, encouraging her with little trills and cries and rubbing reassuringly against her legs. Indeed, her first bath was taken with both of them perched on the toilet seat watching with unblinking intensity every move she made. After a few days her mind regained some measure of normality and she began the task of rebuilding her shattered life, at which point Saki and Lilly relaxed their caution and returned to their old way of life. Emma says now that they were like guardian angels. She has no doubt that without them it would have taken her far longer to recover.

Stories like this are legion: accounts of cats who have

'nursed' their owners through the pain of bankruptcy, divorce and bereavement. A few months ago my friend Jackie suffered her third miscarriage. She recounted how she came back from hospital totally devastated and her five-month-old kitten, Topsy – normally a feline dynamo – spent four whole hours stretched across her belly. For myself, I remember many times when Micia modified her habitually autocratic behaviour out of concern for one of the family. On one unforgettable occasion I sat crying my heart out while she tried to comfort me by rubbing her head against my bare feet.

THE HEALING CAT

Another area where the cat's mysterious powers sometimes manifest is healing. Since the medical profession first recognised their healing abilities in 1970, cats have played an increasingly important role in helping people get over drug and alcohol addiction, as well as being used therapeutically in old people's homes and in schools for the mentally handicapped. Much has been written about the cats who have been instrumental in bringing people out of comas and getting autistic children to speak.

One well-documented case tells the story of a severely autistic American teenager who spent every waking moment staring at a crack on the wall opposite his hospital bed. His parents and doctors had given up any hope of a cure until one of the nurses had the idea of bringing a frolicsome kitten to visit him each day. Several weeks passed before he could tear his eyes from the crack and glance at the animal, but once he did, that was that. The teenager forgot his fixation with the crack. He became totally devoted to the kitten, gradually assuming the responsibility for feeding and grooming him. Eighteen months later, carrying his furry friend in a cat basket, he was able to leave the hospital and attend a school for children with special needs.

One of the most famous 'healing cats' was a marmalade tom who belonged to a lady called Mrs Bailey. She got him from the Cats Protection League in London in the '50s and she named him Rogan. Rogan's singular talent was discovered after an acquaintance of hers sat with him on her lap in the back of a parked car, emerging half an hour later claiming her nervous breakdown miraculously cured. Word soon spread

and people flocked to seek the feline healer's help.
Afflictions as diverse as slipped discs and fading vision
were supposedly cured after a session of 'laying on of
paws'. He also cured Smudgie, a fellow moggie who was
suffering from a form of moggie anorexia, Key-Gaskell
syndrome. As Smudgie lived some distance away, Mrs
Bailey sent combings from Rogan's coat which, once
sniffed, sent Smudgie rushing to his bowl for his first
proper meal in weeks.

This success encouraged Mrs Bailey to send combings
of Rogan's fur to sufferers all over the world. Rogan was
featured in newspapers and magazines and his fame
grew. A Californian radio station interviewed Mrs Bailey
and invited her to take her amazing cat on a US Healing

Tour. A Japanese film crew made a documentary about Rogan, treating him with such deference that they even walked backwards out of his presence.

A little less exotic, perhaps, is an account by a Reverend Wood on the care lavished on him by his cat, Prettina, during a long illness. He wrote:

'It was truly wonderful to note how she learned to know the different hours at which I should take medicine or nourishment; and during the night, if my attendant were asleep, she would call her, and, if she could not wake her without such extreme measures, she would gently nibble the nose of the sleeper, which means never failed to produce the desired effect ... The most marvellous part of this matter was, her never being five minutes wrong in her calculations of the true time, even amid the stillness and darkness of night. But who shall say by what means this little being was enabled to measure the fleeing moments, and by the aid of what power did she connect the lapse of time with the needful attentions of a nurse and her charge? Surely some spirit-guiding power must have animated this sympathetic little creature, and have directed her in her labour of love.'

THE PSYCHIC CAT

Many people hold the opinion that all cats possess a psychic sensibility – that they inhabit realms of occult mystery inaccessible to ordinary human beings. Joseph Banks Rhine, one of the foremost scientists studying animal Extra-Sensory Perception (ESP) in America, has collected over 500 examples of animal behaviour that overwhelmingly indicate ESP. The areas he investigated were:

1) the ability to sense the owner's unexpected return;

2) sensing imminent danger;

3) sensing an owner's death over a distance;

4) the ability to return home across unknown territory;

5) the ability to trace owners who've moved to a new home.

Testimonies to the feline's sixth sense can be found everywhere. For centuries sailors appreciated the presence of the ship's cat, not only because it controlled the rat population, but because they believed it could sense the coming of a storm. Similarly, there are many accounts of war-time cats who, by anticipating an air-raid, enabled their owners to make it to the shelter in the nick of time. Another curious phenomenon is the feline's remarkable grasp of time. Not only do they recognise the chronology of the normal household routine – meal times, time of owner's arrival home, etc – but they also know the different time patterns of a weekend or holiday period.

Foreknowledge of earthquakes is another ability attributed to cats. In his book *Incredible Cats*, David Greene gives the example of the Italian cat, Toto (named after the much-loved Neapolitan comic), who in the middle of the night sensed that Mount Vesuvius was about to erupt. Normally docile, Toto leapt, repeatedly, on his sleeping master, eventually resorting to scratching his cheek. Neapolitans are by nature extremely superstitious. The man's initial fury quickly subsided as he realized his cat's bizarre behaviour could be a warning that danger was imminent. His wife was of the same mind and they immediately evacuated with Toto to relatives living in another part of the region. One hour after their departure Vesuvius did indeed erupt and their village was engulfed by a torrent of incandescent lava.

Also remarkable are the many authenticated instances of cats who have traced their owners across unfamiliar and uncharted territory to a new home. One notable example of this involved a very ordinary little cat called Sugar. Sugar belonged to Stacy Wood, headmaster of a school in Anderson, California. When he retired in 1952 he and his wife moved to a small cattle farm in Cage, Oklahoma. Although the place was ideal for any animal, Sugar was so terrified of travelling that they reluctantly decided it would be kinder to leave her with a neighbour so she could stay in the area she'd always known.

Fourteen months later Stacy and his wife were milking cows in an outhouse when a cat suddenly appeared in one of the windows. It paused for a moment, then leapt onto Mrs Wood's shoulder and began purring like a train. The animal was identical to the pet they'd left behind, but Mr and Mrs Wood were too sensible and down-to-earth to allow themselves to believe it could really be her.

Later, back at the farmhouse, they examined her properly. When they discovered a congenital hip joint deformation they knew without a shadow of a doubt that the new arrival was indeed their Sugar. Mr Wood immediately called the neighbour who was supposed to be looking after her. Rather shamefacedly the neighbour confessed that Sugar had disappeared three weeks after the Woods left town.

The Woods sat down and made some calculations. They worked out that Sugar had been travelling for over a year, during which time she had covered more than 2000 kilometres. How, they asked amazed, had she managed to overcome so many obstacles to track them down to a place she had no way of knowing even existed? A psychic 'homing device of the heart' seemed the only possible explanation.

Toby, the famous train hobo of the feline world, was a traveller of a different sort. As a young kitten he attached himself to the refreshment room at Carlisle station, soon afterwards developing a fascination with rolling stock and a wanderlust that lasted to the end of his days. When he made his first journey nobody knows, but he soon became such a well-known commuter that London Midland Scottish gave him a tag with the message 'If found please return to Carlisle Station' to wear around his neck. The curious thing is that Toby would only take north-bound trains – once making the 245-mile journey to Aberdeen – but, despite tempting bribes of fish by various drivers and guardsmen, he refused to board anything heading south of Carlisle. As for his reasons, we shall never know.

THE RATIONALIST'S VIEW

Not all people, however, believe the cat has psychic powers. These rationalists maintain that the answer to the things we don't understand should be sought, not in the supernatural, but in science. In his book *Catlore*, zoologist and animal behaviourist, Desmond Morris, says that if it could be established that cats are sensitive to minute vibrations or changes in the static electricity of the air around them, then we might understand how it is they predict earthquakes and volcanic eruptions. By the same token he says that if we knew more about their sensitivity to ultrasonic sounds, we might finally fathom how cats 'know' someone is coming even when they are still miles away. And as for the 'psychic trailing', when a cat follows its owners to a new home – well, the answer to that is a combination of wishful thinking and a lookalike stray.

So is the cat mysterious only because we are ignorant or romantic or a mixture of both? Or could it be that there really is something inaccessibly spiritual and arcane in the cat's fundamental nature? My own personal feeling is that only our feline friends know the true answer to that.

Chapter 5

WHAT YOU CAN LEARN FROM YOUR CAT

'There is, indeed, no single quality of the cat that man could not emulate to his advantage. He is clean, the cleanest, indeed, of all animals ... He is silent, entirely self-reliant, beautiful, and graceful. He makes his appearance and his life as exquisite as circumstances will permit. He is modest, he is urbane, he is dignified. A well-bred cat never argues. He goes about doing what he likes in a well-bred, superior manner. If he is interrupted he will look at you in mild surprise or silent reproach but he will return to his desire. If he is prevented, he will wait for a more favourable occasion. But like all well-bred individualists, the cat seldom interferes with other people's rights. His intelligence keeps him from doing many of the fool things that complicate life. Cats never write operas and they never attend them. They never sign papers, or pay taxes, or vote for a president. An injunction will have no power whatever over a cat. A cat, of course, would not only refuse to obey any amendment whatever to any constitution, he would refuse to obey the constitution itself.'

These wise words were written by Carl Van Vechten (1880-1964) in his book *The Tiger in the House*, and I'm sure our feline friends would wholeheartedly agree with him. Certainly Ted would. Ted is a nine-month-old, jet-black tom who believes in cultivating good relations with his immediate neighbours and who visits me regularly. This morning, for example, after the customary ritual of purring, leg-rubbing greeting, he drank a saucer of milk, conducted a sniffing recce of my various houseplants, played a vigorous game with a screwed-up ball of paper, spent several minutes luxuriously stretching and rolling, then curled contentedly on the most comfortable chair and settled down for a snooze.

I observed him with admiration and envy. My own morning had been spent between the phone and the word processor and the only food I'd eaten – toast and Marmite – had been consumed on the trot. My neck muscles were knotted, my head ached and I had failed to noticed that, after two days of sodden rain, a bright December sun was valiantly challenging the heavy cloud.

There was a lesson to be learned from all this, of course, and I recognised it. So following in Ted's pawsteps I, too, made a leisurely tour of the domestic greenery, discovering in the process that two of the avocados were sprouting delicate new leaf. I followed this by doing some stretching exercises, after which I lay down on the carpet and dedicated ten minutes to the relaxation of body and mind. By this time Ted was miaowing by the front door indicating the social call was over and he was ready to go home. I watched him trot off feeling decidedly more invigorated and refreshed than when he had arrived.

HOW TO COPE WITH STRESS

Stress is one of the facts of modern life. No one is completely free from it – indeed, it would be counter-productive if we were. Stress is a double-edged sword. On the positive side it provides the necessary adrenalin for high-performance tasks, on the negative it drains our emotional and physical resources. The important thing, therefore, is to learn to manage stress and avoid building up excessive levels of tension. How we handle stress is crucial to the quality of our life in all its aspects. Indeed, some doctors now take the view that stress management has a direct effect on the actual length of time we live. Successful stress management involves many factors, most importantly recognising one's basic personality type and modifying behaviour accordingly. There is also research showing that people of all types, who may do nothing other than share their homes with animals, tend to live longer than those who don't. One of the many benefits of keeping a pet is that they seem to syphon off accumulated tension. Apart from the fact that just looking at a sleeping puss has a tranquillising effect, it has been medically proven that rhythmically stroking a cat significantly lowers the stroker's blood pressure. This is good news for everybody, of course, but especially for those suffering from clinical hypertension. It is also a well-known fact that cats are wonderfully therapeutic in the treatment of loneliness, depression, anxiety and low self-esteem. While all cat owners have plentiful experience of this, official research has tended to focus on the old, the sick, and those living in institutions.

HOW TO MEDITATE ON LIFE'S FINER POINTS

The cat is a combination of philosopher and laid-back dude. A cat takes time to sit and contemplate. Unlike the human animal – who half the time is blind to the

everyday wonders of his/her immediate environment –
the cat shows intense interest in a fallen leaf, raindrops
racing down a window, the dizzy dance of mating
bluebottles, the fragile green shoots that every
springtime push through the hard crust of wintery
earth. A sense of wonder at nature's miracles is a
precious gift. It is also one of the best antidotes to
modern stress. Indeed, being aware of forces outside
ourselves, of rhythms that are constant despite our own
ups and downs, can give us a larger view on things.
And, just in itself, this is healing.

NODDING OFF: THE BENEFITS OF CATNAPPING

Another enviable feline talent is the ability to nod off at
the drop of a hat – hence the term 'catnap' for a short
sleep. As most of us would benefit from relaxing more
often during the day, this is yet another cat habit well
worth trying to emulate. As any Latin will testify, siestas
are brilliant but most people here just don't have a
lifestyle (or the weather) to accommodate them. On the
other hand, even those with the busiest schedules can
usually manage a few minutes in a quiet corner
dedicated to calm and relaxation. For an effective
'micro-break' sit with eyes closed, head supported, and
concentrate on slow, deep, regular breathing. Place your
hands on your lower ribs to check you are doing it
correctly. With each breath you should feel them
opening out sideways and moving your hands apart.

When the allotted time is up, take a few seconds to refocus before rising to your feet with unhurried, cat-like grace. Learning how to turn a few minutes – even a few seconds – to good use is an effective tool for stress handling and will make all the difference to the quality of your life.

HOW TO STRETCH AND RELAX

The cat is a beautiful and graceful animal. Its body is compact, harmonious, powerful and perfectly balanced. When running its movements are fluid and rhythmical. Curled up into a sleeping ball, it is a picture of sleekly muscled symmetry. And watch the way it stretches when it wakes. It rises with a single vertical thrust, legs straight and its back steeply arched. Then its body arrangement changes again. The fore legs stretch stiffly forward, the paws splay out, the tail-end lifts and the hind legs push backward. Muscles ripple sinuously along the flexible spine and it suddenly looks twice the length it did before.

Cats stretch many times a day and so should we. This means anything from simply lifting our arms above our heads while sitting at a desk to a regular morning routine. Simple stretching exercises help to promote good health and reduce fatigue, thereby boosting our resistance to stress and minor ailments. Practised consistently, they also help strengthen muscles and improve posture. The following are basic yoga-type stretch exercises of which your cat will most certainly approve.

STRETCH 1 (STRAIGHT)

Stand with the outer edges of your bare feet parallel and your big toes touching. Stretch your toes fully and take the weight evenly on both feet. Once your feet feel firmly rooted to the floor, lift up from your arches and stretch through your legs, pulling up your kneecaps by tightening your front thigh muscles. Tighten your buttock muscles and tuck in your tailbone. Lift your ribs, drop your shoulders and let your arms hang loosely. Extend your neck without lifting your chin or pulling it in too far. You should feel as though someone is pulling you up by an invisible cord attached to the crown of your head. While you hold this basic stretch, breathe slowly and easily.

STRETCH 2 (SIDEWAYS)

Stand tall, stretching up through your spine, as in
Stretch 1. Spread your feet as wide apart as you can
whilst maintaining a secure balance. Place your left
hand on your waist, stretch your right arm up towards
the ceiling, then stretch sideways to the left as far as
you can go without straining. Remember to keep your
tailbone well tucked in and your buttock muscles
clenched. Repeat on the other side.

STRETCH 3 (FORWARD)

Once again stand tall as in Stretch 1. Then spread your
feet as wide apart as you can with your toes pointing
forward. Bend your elbows and put your hands on your
hips. Keeping your legs straight, bend forward from the
hips, trying to make your body as parallel as possible
with the floor.

STRETCH 4 (CAT STRETCH)

Kneel on all fours, knees hip-width apart and arms shoulder-width apart. Lift your head and your tailbone towards the ceiling (keeping knees and hands securely on the floor) so that your back dips into a hollow. Then lower your head to look at your navel, clench your buttock muscles to pull your tailbone in, and arch your back like a Hallowe'en cat. Keep your movements smooth and repeat several times.

Chapter 6

KEEPING HEALTHY TOGETHER

DIET AND LIFESTYLE

The cat is a carnivore and its natural food is prey. This means birds, fish, insects, reptiles and small mammals, especially rodents, which provide not only raw meat, but also roughage in the form of skin, fur and bones. Cats are not by nature overeaters, and in the wild they efficiently regulate the amount of food they take in. A fully-grown cat needs from four to seven ounces of food a day. Some prefer this served up as two meals of smaller (mouse-sized?) portions, while others like tucking into one substantial meal. It's a good idea to introduce a variety of foods as soon as they are weaned. This ensures a balanced diet and – just as important – helps to prevent Puss or Felix becoming the sort of feline food faddist who stages an immediate hunger strike if their owner fails to provide them with the exact brand/meat/flavour they want. In my experience, this common form of blackmail almost always works.

WHY CAN'T HE BE A VEGETARIAN?

Good nutrition is as essential to feline health as it is to human health. While we might benefit from all sorts of curious and exotic diets, a cat most certainly does not. This is particularly true of a vegetarian or vegan diet. There are several reasons for this. Firstly, unlike all other animals, the feline metabolism cannot synthesise Vitamin A and they must get it from liver, kidney and fish oils. Deprived of Vitamin A they suffer weight loss, night blindness, a greater susceptibility to infection and possibly infertility. Cats are also unable to manufacture the amino-acid, taurine, which they obtain exclusively from animal proteins and without which severe deterioration of the retinas would occur. Finally, cats

need animal fats because they lack the ability to convert vegetable oils into essential fatty acids.

For a correct proportion of proteins, fats, carbohydrates, minerals and vitamins, cats need a high-protein, high-fat diet. Most of the commercially-produced food on the market is excellent but it's good to serve fresh food, too. Cheap cuts of beef and lamb, boned or diced rabbit, poultry, offal, fish and cheese are alternatives your cat will welcome. Egg yolks are also nourishing and can be served beaten into milk. A word of caution about milk, however. An adult cat should not drink too much, as over-indulgence can give rise to digestive problems. (Indeed, some doctors and nutritionists say the same is true for us.) It's worth bearing in mind that milk is more of a food than a drink and, when your cat is thirsty, it should have water.

Although a totally vegetarian diet is out, plant-based foods can form part of a cat's eating regime. In fact, many cats are are quite partial to cooked greens and digest them easily. Try Puss with a few boiled vegetables such as cabbage, carrots, peas, broad and runner beans, chopped up and mixed with meat, breakfast cereals like wheatflakes, puffed rice and even mashed potatoes.

The natural way for a cat to live is outdoors and hunting. (Although as Christopher Day points out in the introduction to his book *Natural Remedies for Your Cat*, outdoor life has its own hazards in the form of traffic, dogs, birds of prey, other cats, etc.) In the natural environment a cat finds the grass it needs to ingest to clear its intestines of fur balls, as well as for an occasional purge. So if your cat doesn't have access to an outside lawn, grow a nice big pot of grass indoors.

OBESITY

Obesity has been an increasing problem for people in the affluent West for many years. Now, it seems, we are passing that problem on to our cats. A recent American study found that as much as a third of all pet cats are overweight. One reason for this is that pet food has become such a delicious gourmet treat that the animals gorge. Another is that owners too often express their love by over-feeding. It's a natural instinct to want to indulge and pamper those we love. Indeed, some people are actually proud of their heavyweight moggies because it shows how adored and spoilt they are. The

plain truth is, however, that a fat cat is an unhealthy cat and the sooner it loses its extra pounds the better.

How much and what we feed our cat is likely to reflect our attitudes to food generally. If we are overeaters ourselves, for example, then we are more likely to encourage a greedy cat. Puss might thoroughly enjoy a chocolate truffle or a nice, ripe bit of brie and, for the occasional treat, that's just fine. What we must never forget, however, is that what's good for Puss and what's good for us is not the same thing. Taking a fresh look at Puss's nutrition is an opportunity to correct bad eating habits – including some of our own!

RECOGNISING WHEN YOUR CAT IS ILL

A healthy cat is easy to recognise. The coat is well-groomed and glossy, the eyes bright, free of discharge and with no third-eyelid protrusion, the ears are clean and the breath odourless. The cat is neither too thin nor too fat and behaves with the curiosity and liveliness appropriate to its personality and age.

The cat is a superb animal. Evolution has given it a sleek hunter's body which combines grace with strength and flexibility. The efficiency of feline physiology has allowed it to adapt to a variety of climates, thrive on a wide range of foodstuffs and develop an excellent resistance to infections. Furthermore, wounds to the surface of its skin heal with an astounding rapidity.

Like all living creatures, however, cats get sick too,

and it is important to recognise the signs. The problem for us – and for the vet – is that, vocal though they often are, they do not have the language to tell us how they feel. In practice, a caring, attentive owner soon notices any changes indicating that something is wrong. Physical signs can include lumps, cuts, runny eyes, scabs, weight loss, diarrhoea or evidence of pain. Behavioural signs might be lack of appetite, excessive drinking, listlessness or anything that indicates the cat is not feeling its usual self.

The caring, attentive owner who knows his cat well can confidently treat minor ailments and administer basic first aid at home. If symptoms persist, however, or the illness seems more serious, it is important to seek veterinary attention right away.

THE VET

All vets must be fully qualified and registered. As a general rule, it's a good idea to choose one near to where you live, so if an emergency arises you can reach the surgery easily and without delay. Nowadays it is common for several veterinarians to share a practice and work on a rota system. Although these large practices often have a wider range of specialist equipment and facilities, some people prefer the personal attention and continuity a small practice can offer. For routine treatments, such as innoculations, it doesn't really matter if you see a different vet each time. But when a cat falls ill, it is natural to feel more reassured if the vet is the same. If the surgery is a large one, enquire if your cat can receive treatment by the same vet in the event of illness.

Some practices operate under an appointments-only system. Others hold regular open surgeries, where you can just turn up and take your turn in the queue. When checking these things out, consider also the overall atmosphere of the place. Are the staff friendly and helpful, for example? Do you feel generally comfortable with the way the surgery is run? In health care, both our own and that of our felines, these aspects play an important role.

Veterinarians can be found listed in the *Yellow Pages* or through advertisements. Best of all, however, is personal recommendation from a pet-owning friend or neighbour. Costs do vary and veterinary bills can be quite expensive. For people who are on benefit, animal charities like the PDSA, RSPCA, CPL and the Blue Cross Animal Hospitals will carry out treatment, asking only for a donation towards the cost.

For those who prefer the alternative approach to medicine, details of The British Association of Homoeopathic Veterinary Surgeons and names and addresses of veterinary surgeons can be obtained from The Homoeopathic Development Foundation Ltd in London.

ALTERNATIVE FIRST AID

HOMOEOPATHY

Homoeopathy is a natural healing process that provides remedies to stimulate the body's natural recovery mechanism. Derived from the Greek word *homoios*, meaning 'like', homoeopathy is based on a law of nature (known since the time of the Ancient Greeks), namely that like cures like. It was divised almost 200 years ago by the German physician, Christian Hahnemann, who found the medical practices of his time completely unacceptable. During tests, Dr Hahnemann discovered that by taking small doses of cinchona bark (quinine) he could produce in himself mild symptoms of malaria.

And if similar doses were given to people actually suffering from malaria, they were cured. He explained it thus: 'Each disease is most safely, quickly and comfortably cured by the remedy – in minute doses – which, given in large doses, produces a reaction in the healthy body that most closely resembles the symptoms in question.'

Conventional medicine takes the view that the symptoms are a direct manifestation of the illness, whereas homoeopathy sees the symptoms as the organism reacting against the illness it is trying to fight. Its task, therefore, is to strengthen and not repress this reaction by the administration of substances which boost the body's own defence mechanisms. Surprisingly, it was found that the more diluted the remedy, the more powerful its effect.

Since its discovery, homoeopathy has cured many millions of people. Homoeopathic medicines are used the world over and are recognised as an effective alternative to conventional remedies. They are prepared from pure, natural sources and, because the doses are so small, there is no risk of overdosing, poisoning or other such side-effects – in other words, they are completely safe. In recent years homoeopathy has been used increasingly, and equally effectively, in the treatment of animals. This has confounded those critics who sought to explain the success of homoeopathy as simply auto-suggestion. If people believe they will be cured, they argued, then their minds will trigger a reaction in their body. Obviously, this can't be the case with animals.

For any condition that is serious, or even just the slightest bit puzzling, one should always consult a veterinary surgeon. First aid and the treatment of straightforward ailments, however, can usually be competently dealt with at home. A number of the most common cat illnesses and conditions and the appropriate homoeopathic remedies are listed below.

How to Give Treatment
All medicines should be given in tablet form unless otherwise stated. The ideal method of administration is to pulverise the tablet and sprinkle it directly onto the cat's tongue when it's not eating. If the cat resists, however, dissolve the powder in milk or water or mix it with a little food.

Dosage
Acute conditions may require one dose every hour for three or four doses. For less acute conditions, give one once or twice a day for a few days. Chronic conditions may need treatment only once per week or even less.

There are a variety of potencies. In general, 6c is the potency appropriate for home treatment.

Storage
Homoeopathic medicines should be kept in a cool, dry place away from sunlight, strong perfumes, camphor, disinfecting agents, or similar substances. Stored this way, remedies will retain their potency for many years.

Although I have concentrated on homoeopathic remedies because they are safe and easy to administer, I have also mentioned some other alternative remedies:

HERBAL REMEDIES

These are not as diluted as homoeopathic ones, and so they should be given with caution. Infusions of herbs are made by pouring boiling water over the plant – use one teaspoon of herbs per teacup of water, and this gives ten doses of herbal medicine. You can also buy tinctures or powders of herbs. Two or three drops of tincture or a pinch of powder is enough for one dose.

BACH FLOWER REMEDIES

These are prepared from wild flowers. They are stored in alcohol or water and should be given orally.

THE SKIN

Abscess

An abscess results from an open wound which has gone untreated. Because feline skin heals so quickly, infective organisms sometimes become trapped, causing an abscess to develop. When an abscess bursts, there is a discharge of smelly, blood-streaked pus from the abscess cavity.

Treatment: before it bursts, use Hepar sulphuris. Once the abscess bursts, first bathe with a weak solution of salt and boiling water (half a teaspoon of salt to 2 litres

(1 pint) of water) that has been allowed to cool to blood
temperature, then dose with Silica.

Abrasions

Bathe the broken skin with a solution of Hypercal
mother tincture. Treat with Hypericum.

Dandruff

Dandruff is the formation of loose scales of dead skin.
Try changing your cat's diet, avoiding dry food
altogether for a while, and keep the coat regularly
brushed.

For dry, scaly skin: Arsenicum album.

For red skin: Sulphur.

Eczema

Eczema is a skin inflammation with lesions that scale,
crust or ooze a thin, watery fluid.

For dry, cracked skins: Natrum muriaticum.

For red skin: Sulphur.

For wet, weeping sores and for sticky discharge:
Graphites.

For scabby skin: Mezereum alternated with Petroleum.

Fleas

Cats are prone to parasite infestations. Fleas are most
commonly found on the neck, back, haunches and
around the tail area. While treating your animal, it is
important not to forget to disinfect all the dark corners
and crannies where fleas lay their eggs. Fleas appear as

small black points on the cat's skin and are easy to recognise. Try covering your cat with commercially-available flea powder, then immediately wrap it up in a blanket or pillowcase so only the head sticks out. Afterwards, stand the cat on newspaper and give its fur a thorough brush. Take care when disposing of the paper, as fleas do not die immediately.

To strengthen protective coating of the skin: Sulphur.

EYES, EARS AND MOUTH

Bad Breath
Bad breath is generally caused by decaying teeth or an accumulation of tartar, and needs to be treated by a veterinarian. There is no natural remedy to prevent the formation of tartar.

Before the appointment to help heal any extractions: Arnica.

When it's due to gastric upset: Carbo Veg or Nux Vom.

Conjunctivitis
Conjunctivitis is an inflammation of the delicate, mucous membrane that covers the eyeball.

For a simple, uncomplicated condition: Argent. Nit. or Pulsatilla.

If there is discharge: Euphrasia.

Eye, Eyelid or Cheek
Injuries in the vicinity of the eye, eyelid or cheek are

frequently caused by fighting. Wash the wound three or four times a day with 20 drops of Calendula tincture in one cup of warm water.

To aid healing: Hepar sulphuris.

Ear Conditions
Cats often have trouble with their ears, frequently caused by ear mites living in the wax. An afflicted cat will shake its head a lot and constantly scratch behind the ears.

Acutely inflamed and sensitive: Hepar sulphuris.

Discharge with garlic odour: Arsenicum album.

Suppurating with foul-smelling discharge: Mercurius solubilis.

Chronic cases: Rhus Tox.

RESPIRATORY TRACT

Colds, Coughs, Catarrh etc
As cats are very susceptible to these conditions, more than a couple of sneezes should have the alert cat owner reaching for the Aconitum. A few timely doses of Aconitum should not only stop the cold, but should cure it. In the case of suspected cat flu, veterinary advice should be sought immediately. A cat that is coming down with cat flu will be obviously unwell, eating little and almost certainly running a temperature. Frequent doses of Belladonna will help bring down the temperature, making the cat feel more

comfortable.

For hard dry coughs: Phosphorus.

Worse when animal moves: Bryonia.

Accompanied by palpitations of the heart: Drosera.

Catarrh and sinusitis: Kali bich.

DIGESTIVE ORGANS

Constipation

It is mostly old cats that suffer from constipation.
Raw liver, milk, cream or sardine oil can relieve the
complaint. A tablespoon of warm olive oil added to food
will also help, as will brushing the cat and coaxing it
into being more active.

Simple, uncomplicated constipation: Nux Vom. or
Carbo Veg. These remedies also relieve colic and
flatulence.

Diarrhoea

Diarrhoea is an inflammation of the bowel and can be
caused by a virus or bacteria, chemical irritants in food,
or infection by micro-organisms or worms. If infectious
feline enteritis is suspected you should take your cat
immediately to the vet. Less severe conditions can be
treated at home.

Watery stools with gastric symptoms: Arsenicum
album or Arnica.

Slimy, blood-stained or watery, explosive stools:
Mercurius solubilis.

If the cat has overeaten – a whole chicken for example – Nux vomica is recommended.

Worms
Roundworm: Abrotanum. Tapeworm: Cina. Hookworms: Carduus marianus. Garlic also deals effectively with all parasites and can given mixed up in food.

Vomiting
Cats have a strong vomiting reflex which allows them to rid their bodies quickly of any harmful substance they might have eaten. Cats vomit after eating grass to remove hairballs from the stomach (excessive grass eating, however, might indicate something more serious and should be checked out by a vet) and if they have eaten too quickly or the food was too cold.

Simple vomiting after indigestible food: Ipecacuanha.

INFECTIOUS DISEASES

Like all living creatures, cats are vulnerable to dangerous viruses and bacteria. Diseases in this category include Feline Leukaemia (FeLV), Feline Distemper, Toxoplasmosis, and Feline AIDS (FTLV). These are all extremely serious and need to be treated by a vet.

SHOCK

A cat can go into shock for a variety of reasons. These include a fall from a window, an attack by an aggressive dog and, of course, road accidents. Physical symptoms of shock are a fast heartbeat, breathing in short, shallow gasps, a lowering of temperature, possibly spontaneous vomiting or excretion, and the gums and inside of eyelids turning pale. Even if there are no apparent injuries, it is advisable to have your cat seen by a veterinarian as quickly as possible. Meanwhile keep the cat warm with a hot water bottle wrapped in a blanket and talk reassuringly in a soothing, soft tone.

Immediately after the incident: Aconite.

Although effective, Aconite is short-lasting. Follow it up with Arnica.

Rescue Remedy, a Bach flower remedy, is also excellent for treating shock.

ZOONOSES

This word refers to any infections or diseases that are transmitted from animals to people. The risks are usually extremely small, but it is sensible to be vigilant.

Toxoplasmosis

Toxoplasmosis in humans and in other animals has been known about for over 70 years. When a cat is first infected it passes the organisms in its faeces. If the excrement is not removed, the little cysts on the surface of the faeces dry up and become particles in the air that we breathe. In the case of a farm cat, the disease is introduced into the food chain thus: a cat deposits its faeces in cattle feed; the cattle then eats the feed and absorbs the organisms into its muscle; we eat the cattle in the form of meat and become infected in turn. A person can also become infected by handling cat faeces or garden soil where a cat may have defecated.

Toxoplasmosis generally causes symptoms similar to a dose of flu. It is extremely dangerous for pregnant women, however, as the parasite can enter the foetus and cause brain damage. A pregnant woman, therefore, should take the following precautions:

1) always eat meat well cooked;

2) wear gloves when cleaning out the litter tray, or, better still, get someone else to do it;

3) have the cat checked by a veterinarian for toxoplasmosis.

Toxocariasis (Roundworm)
Most kittens are infected with roundworms from their mother's milk as soon as they have suckled. In the larval stage, cat roundworm can infect humans, inducing a condition known as visceral larva migrans, which can cause damage to the eyes. Have your cat regularly dewormed and observe hygiene precautions when handling cat faeces.

Ringworm

This is a fungal disease characterised by round, red patches on the skin, sometimes with crusty scabs. Ringworm is usually only transmitted to those people who are susceptible to it. In such cases it manifests as circular patches of thickened, reddish skin, usually on the hands and forearms as they are the parts of the body which have most contact with the cat. Ringworm is not a very serious disease and responds well to conventional and alternative forms of treatment.

ALLERGIES

Allergies are the most common physical problem associated with keeping a cat. Some people know they are allergic from childhood, others begin manifesting allergic reactions out of the blue in adult life. Streaming eyes, running nose and swollen eyelids are classic symptoms that can sometimes be relieved by taking antihistamine drugs. An even more serious symptom is asthma. Asthma is a chronic condition which produces attacks of breathlessness and wheezing that can last anything from a few hours to several days. It is a particularly distressing condition for a child and the reason why many parents feel forced to ban animals from the house. There are those, however, who are all too aware of the emotional damage they inflict when removing a beloved cat from an allergic and asthmatic child, so much so that some parents decide to favour the child's emotional wellbeing and let the animal stay.

But hyper-allergic cat lovers need not despair. In his book *Catlore*, Desmond Morris suggests two breeds they can happily share their home with. The Rex or 'Poodle cat' was developed from a curly-coated kitten found by the English cat expert, Sidney Denham, in Cornwall in 1950. It has a short, sparse, curly coat lacking the usual long guard hairs and crinkly whiskers that are presumed to cause the allergic reactions in humans. Although of odd appearance (it is often described as having a pixie face), the Rex retains a delightfully friendly and kittenish personality in its adult life.

The Sphinx Cat – the most perfect cat from an anti-allergic point of view – has an even more bizarre appearance. Developed from a hairless kitten born in Canada in 1966, the body of an adult Sphinx is almost entirely bald, retaining the short, soft down it is born with only on its face and extremities. As it moves its naked skin wrinkles and creases in a way many people find disturbing. Indeed, it has the reputation for being the ugliest feline in the world. There are those, however, who disagree, and the Sphinx has a growing number of fans. Desmond Morris suggests making it a coat of some non-allergic material, both to cover its unfamiliar nudity and to keep it warm.

THE GREEN CAT

In 1987, pets in the UK consumed 651,000 tonnes of

food, most of it fish- or meat-based. This means that many other animals have been slaughtered to feed them, a fact which can be hard to accept for the owner who is vegetarian. In her book *Home Ecology: Making Your World a Better Place*, Karen Christensen mentions that in America the giant Blue Bass was hunted to near extinction in order to satisfy the appetites of the dog and cat population. She also points out that tuna fishing – tuna being used a lot in commercial cat food – causes the death of thousands of dolphins. Another environmental cost of pet-keeping is the packaging.

According to the Green Consumer Guide, 80 per cent of owners buy tinned pet food, which adds up to a staggering 2 billion pet-food cans to be disposed of per year.

Karen Christensen suggests that the first thing a Green Cat Owner should do is wean their feline off commercial pet foods. Packets and tins are not only expensive and wasteful, she says, but they might also be damaging your cat's health. The reason for this is that, like processed human food, the contents are heavily laced with chemical additives and added flavourings such as salt and sugar. There is also a risk that the lead from soldering may have contaminated the food. As even the Vegetarian Society agrees that vegetarianism is inappropriate for cats, Karen Christensen suggests a diet most closely resembling the one the animal would have in the wild: raw meat and fresh offal.

The Green Cat Owner should also avoid anti-flea shampoos, sprays, powders or collars. They all contain extremely toxic pesticides incorporating substances such as chlorinated insecticide, of which the hazardous Lindane is the most active ingredient. If you have your home fumigated against a flea infestation, for example, check what pesticides are being used and vacate the home for several days.

The non-toxic approach set out in Karen Christensen's book is painstakingly to vacuum carpets, rugs, upholstery, cushions, mattresses – in fact, everything that is vacuumable – and dispose of the vacuum bag by sealing it in a plastic bag or burning it. The next step is to add brewer's yeast or a crushed clove of garlic to Puss's food each day. The yeast and garlic have the effect of making her smell unappetising to parasites, and garlic is also recommended for worms.

A herb called Pennyroyal, however, is the chief
weapon in the Great Flea War and Karen Christensen
suggests making a flea collar by packing a roll of fabric
with dried Pennyroyal leaves or giving the cat a bath
with a strong Pennyroyal infusion. Pennyroyal oil is
available from herbalists and can be rubbed on an
existing leather collar and sprinkled on the cat's
bedding. It seems, however, that Pennyroyal has in
rare cases caused spontaneous abortion, and Karen
Christensen cautions to be careful with a pregnant cat.

THE OLD CAT

The old cat appears in this chapter because, although
not ill necessarily, the time has come when he or she
needs extra understanding and consideration. Over the
years a deep and special bond has been created, and we
honour that bond with the quality of our care.

Once Puss has reached the age of 14 she can start to
be considered elderly. Felines show their age less
obviously than humans (no wrinkles or dewlaps, for
example!), but they are certainly less active. They play
less, spend more time asleep, and show less inclination
to wander far from home. In some cats there is a loss of
coat colour, and others grey a little around the muzzle,
although it's extremely rare for felines to become more
grizzled than that. In fact, some Siamese cats actually
turn darker.

Old cats, like old people, appreciate their creature

comforts. They welcome special pampering and are entitled to have their whims indulged every now and then. The fussy eater will become even more finicky with age, while those who in youth were uncomplaining, grow more difficult to please. To stimulate an old Puss's flagging appetite give her the occasional culinary treat, as well as heating food to blood temperature to enhance the taste.

My friend Ruth has a 21-year-old Tortoiseshell whose appetite diminished to the point where she was eating practically nothing. To tickle her taste buds, Ruth concocted a dish of gently poached cod and chicken livers, mixed with half a teaspoon of ketchup and a drop of cod liver oil. It did the trick, and Bambi now tucks into this delicacy every day, followed by the saucer of sweet, milky tea which is her passion. 'I treat her the way I hope someone will treat me when I'm an old lady,' Ruth says, 'and Bambi couldn't be more content.'

Whether they be feline or human, old bones feel the cold more acutely than young bones do. For Micia, warmth had always come high on her list of priorities and we sometimes felt guilty for having deprived her of an old age basking luxuriously in the Roman sun. To make up for this, each morning one of us would prepare her favourite chair with two hot water bottles covered by the crocheted blanket that had been hers since kittenhood. During the last six months of her life she spent much time curled up there, yowling with surprised indignation when the water in the bottles began to cool. Because we lived in a flat, Micia only had a short stroll to the bathroom when she wanted to use her litter tray. Many older cats with gardens, however, are often understandably reluctant to venture out on cold or wet nights when nature calls. An indoor litter tray for emergency use would be something I'm sure these senior citizens would appreciate.

Old age is a slowing down. It is also a time when the odd eccentric behaviour might manifest. By accepting this we can show love, respect and consideration for the feline who has been our treasured and long-standing companion.

ON A CAT AGEING

Sir Alexander Gray, Scottish professor and poet:

He blinks upon the hearth rug
And yawns in deep content,
Accepting all the comforts
That Providence has sent.

Louder he purrs and louder,
In one glad hymn of praise
For all the night's adventures,
For quiet, restful days.

Life will go on forever,
With all that cat can wish;
Warmth, and the glad procession
Of fish and milk and fish.

Only – the thought disturbs him -
He's noticed once or twice,
That times are somehow breeding
A nimbler race of mice.

Chapter 7

DEATH AND BEREAVEMENT

Because of the advances of medical science, human beings today live significantly longer and healthier lives – and so do well-cared-for cats. Three hundred years ago Edward Topsell wrote, 'The females live not above five or seven yeares, the males live longer especially if they be gelt.' By 1969 the feline lifespan had increased to between ten and 12 years and nowadays your average moggie can expect to be around for 15 to 17 years. Indeed, one even hears of cats surviving into their 20s and 30s. Remarkable and reassuring though this is, however, it does not alter the fact that a cat's life is considerably shorter than our own. However hard we try to accept this reality, it is always painful when the time comes. In fact, this difference in life expectancy is the single most difficult aspect of the feline/human relationship.

The death of a loved one, be it human or animal, is a life tragedy and evokes emotions of sorrow, desolation and despair. The intensity of our grief is determined, not by species, but by the degree of love and dependency that particular relationship involved. But while the nature of grief is the same, the outlet which society and our culture provide for its expression is not. Human death is surrounded by both practicalities (funeral arrangements, sorting out of personal effects, etc) and symbolic ritual. Relatives, friends, neighbours and work colleagues can usually be counted on to rally round with compassion and support. It is understood that a bereaved person might need to share his or her feelings, that to express emotion is healthier than bottling it up. Those who for some reason or other feel their immediate support system is inadequate, can seek the help of a minister of religion, a sympathetic GP or a bereavement counsellor.

With the death of a pet, however, the situation is very different. There is no funeral, no letters of condolence, no flowers, no formalised mourning. Worse still, there is little understanding for the depth and complexity of the griever's despair. If anything, people tend to be embarrassed by overt displays of anguish over what was 'only an animal, after all'.

This was the experience of Dorothy, whose beautiful Blue Persian, Gigi, died aged 19. Initially sympathetic, her partner of four years soon became exasperated at what he saw as a 'completely over-the-top reaction'. That she could become so upset over the death of a 'mere cat', was to him a sign of her emotional instability. He kept telling her to pull herself together. Anyone would think she was some lonely old spinster, he said, not a successful potter blessed with a man who loved her and a delightful toddler son.

It took Dorothy nine months to fully recover from Gigi's death. During that time she felt her grief was cutting her off from the rest of the world. She began suffering from headaches and dry, reddish patches appeared all over her face and body. Her doctor, sensing an emotional cause behind these symptoms, asked if she was worried or upset about anything. Dorothy refused to confide in him, however, because she believed he would dismiss her as a 'neurotic' if she mentioned Gigi.

Her inner healing started when she began writing thoughts and feelings about the death in a notebook.

Later she became friendly with a neighbour who was grieving for her own cat recently killed by a car. Talking to someone who had been through a similar experience and externalising her emotions allowed Dorothy to finally put Gigi's death behind her.

DOUBLE MOURNING

Julian was similarly affected when Hollywood, brother of Frankie, died of what the vet said afterwards was cat flu. He expired, covered by a blanket on the living room sofa, less than 24 hours after manifesting the first symptoms. Unlike Dorothy, Julian was not concerned about lack of emotional support – indeed, he didn't want to talk about his grief. In his case, what made things worse was the feeling that he'd been somehow negligent and at fault. He berated himself for not having immediately recognised the severity of the situation, for not having taken him immediately to the vet.

Guilt frequently accompanies bereavement: guilt at things said or done, guilt at having been helpless in the face of illness, guilt even for still being alive when the loved one is dead. Frankie and Hollywood were six-week-old kittens when Julian and Silvia brought them home. Frankie was Julian's cat, Hollywood was Silvia's, and together they symbolised the relationship itself. Several months earlier Silvia had moved out. Although it was an amicable separation, Hollywood's death released feelings of guilt over the breakup that Julian had never fully acknowledged. In effect, he was grieving for both the death of Hollywood the cat, and for the 'dead' relationship that Hollywood represented.

'Double mourning' occurs when the normal grieving process (over death, divorce, a major disappointment, etc) is repressed, only to manifest – often with a vengeance – at the next crisis. When Karen's much-loved father died of prostate cancer she appeared to cope extremely well. As well as making all the funeral arrangements, she was a pillar of strength to her mother and younger siblings. In the following months she worked harder than ever at her job, as well as throwing herself into fund-raising activities for cancer research. And then six months later her cat died and this time she just fell apart. Fortunately, a friend managed to persuade her to seek professional help. Karen began twice-weekly sessions with a counsellor who helped her confront the emotional pain of both her losses.

DEATH AND GROWING UP

For many children their first encounter with death is when the family pet dies. It is a distressing experience and one which can also be very frightening. One moment the world is solid, fixed and dependable, the next it has become destabilised by the concept of impermanency. The RSPCA pamphlet *When Your Pet Dies* offers the following advice on helping children over the loss:

1) always tell the truth;

2) let children see you upset can encourage them to express their own feelings;

3) talk about the pet, but concentrate on the good times;

4) if you lost an animal when you were young, tell your children how you felt. Try not to tell them how they should be feeling, however;

5) help your children understand they are not to blame for the pet's death;

6) don't talk about getting a new pet too soon. Your child will need time to get over the death of the old pet.

The death of an animal to a child on the threshold of young adulthood has further significance. As Aaron Katcher says, 'The death of a pet becomes a kind of rite of passage, a symbol of the loss of animal innocence, animal itself.' This was true for Danny whose cat, Sylvester, died the year he turned 17. Sylvester was a year older than Danny and had always been in his life.

He was his friend, his confidante, his comforter, his ally. He was the warm, cuddly presence that had shared his bed ever since he could remember. On a scale of 0-10, Danny rates the pain he felt at Sylvester's death at '10 and over'. It was the deepest unhappiness he had ever known and totally obliterated his suffering over a girl who had recently dumped him. 'He was part of me and I was part of him,' he says. 'We had a real symbiosis. He was there at every stage of my growing up and when he died, that carefree, trusting, part of my childhood was over.'

DEATH AND THE ELDERLY

One of the biggest social changes of 20th-century Britain is the disintegration of the extended family. Gone are the days when uncles, aunts, cousins and grandparents were a structural, interactive part of everybody's life. Furthermore, over the last 20 years the nuclear family has been fast disintegrating too. As a direct result of this, more than one person in ten in the UK now lives alone, and of these, many are elderly. Old age brings many problems, and loneliness can be one of the worst. Friends and contemporaries die, children and grandchildren leave home and move away. The human being is a social animal and his well-being depends of a sense of belonging and purpose. In our society, however, many old people have no role to play in the fast-moving world beyond their door.

In this context, the companionship of a pet assumes
enormous importance. It brings life, warmth, affection
and acceptance into an otherwise isolated and
emotionally-deprived world. We all need to love and be
loved. We all need to touch and be touched. A pet fulfils
a basic human need for something to love, nurture,
caress and hold. Looking after an animal makes a
person feel that they are necessary, that they matter.

It gives structure and purpose to the day, thereby
boosting morale and self-esteem. A pet also offers a link
with the wider world of animal lovers with whom the
elderly person can find much of common interest to
talk about.

The anxiety of the elderly is not that their cat will die before them, but that they will die before their cat. Worry over what will happen to their pet in the event of their having an accident, going into hospital, or dying is something that preys on many minds. The Cats Protection League recommends establishing an emergency arrangement for looking after the cat as soon as it is first acquired (although it's never too late, of course) – possibly a friend, relative or reliable neighbour. It is important to carry a personal emergency card which will inform the emergency services or hospital staff of the arrangements. These cards can be obtained free of charge by sending a stamped, self-addressed envelope to The Cats Protection League, whose address you will find in the back of thisbook.

EUTHANASIA

The single thing that most distinguishes feline death from human death is the extensive use of euthanasia. Euthanasia (also called mercy-killing) is the painless killing of a living creature, usually to relieve suffering from an incurable illness. This is done by injecting a concentrated form of anaesthetic into a vein. Unconsciousness is instantaneous and death follows within seconds. Bruce Fogel talks much about the subject in his book *Pets and Their People*. Helping owners make a life-and-death decision over their pet's fate is, he says, unique to veterinary medicine and the part of his practice he finds most difficult. For most people, euthanasia is a heartbreaking choice made in response to a hopeless situation. There are, however, those who ask the vet to kill their animal for the most trivial and unacceptable reasons. As a guideline, Bruce Fogel sets out the following as valid reasons for ending an animal's life:

1) overwhelming physical injury;
2) irreversible disease that has progressed to a point where distress or discomfort cannot be controlled;
3) old age wear-and-tear that permanently effect the 'quality of life';
4) physical injury, disease or wear-and-tear resulting in permanent loss of control of body functions;
5) aggressiveness with risk to children, owners or others;
6) the carrying of untreatable disease dangerous to humans (for example, rabies).

Everybody would like their cat to die naturally of old age and the decision to euthanise is always a hard one. Any guilt feelings are inevitably magnified and make the sorrow even more acute. Many owners choose to stay with their cat, talking to or stroking it while the injection is administered. This can be emotionally helpful as it allows the person to show love to his or her animal right up to the very end. Very importantly, it also reassures them that the death is as swift and peaceful as promised.

I was present when Micia was euthanised, as were both of my sons. She was suffering from kidney failure and the sympathetic Australian vet told us there was nothing to be done. Afterwards we stood on the pavement with the empty cat basket, hugging each other and crying. The fact that it was raining and Micia had been an Italian cat who loved warmth and sun seemed somehow symbolic. Her death felt unreal. She had been with us for so long that it took several weeks before the reality of it sunk in. We were comforted by the fact she had been spared prolonged suffering and that we were with her when her time came.

SPIRITUALITY

For most people, death and spirituality are inextricably linked. With the destruction of the physical body comes an end to all provable certainties. Death reminds us that a heartbeat is all that separates a living being from the fathomless black void. Death is the ultimate enigma. It arouses both the deepest fear and the keenest fascination. From the beginning of history, wise men and holy men have been driven to discover what lies beyond the grave. This great quest – which is still evolving – has given us the concepts of heaven, hell, nirvana, and the various forms of afterlife.

The Catholic religion says animals have no souls and, therefore, no spiritual life. For the Catholic Church, an animal's existence is limited to the corporeal one. Saint

Ambrose disagreed, however. He was a distinguished lawyer who lived in Italy during the fourth century, becoming a Roman Catholic priest and later bishop of Milan. In his sermons he preached that this dogma was wrong and had resulted in a great deal of cruelty being inflicted on the animal world. He pleaded with the faithful to ignore the teaching and to treat animals with respect and kindness.

The ancient Egyptians, of course, took a very different view to the Catholic Church. The cat was a lunar symbol, sacred to the goddess Isis, and in that guise is sometimes depicted on top of the sistrum Isis holds in her hands. Cats were expected to go to the same afterworld as human beings, and food to sustain them on their journey was always buried with them.

Spiritualists also believe animals inhabit a realm beyond death. Many accounts of ghostly cats have appeared in the publications *Psychic News* and *Proceedings of the Society for Psychical Research*. In a typical report of 1884, a Mrs Griefenberg and her daughter claimed to have seen a large white Angora cat with green eyes under the table where they were having lunch. The women followed it out of the room and into the passageway. Halfway along, the cat turned to stare at them and then dissolved into thin air. To psychics, these phantom manifestations point to the existence of a spirit world parallel to our own.

The Buddhist view is that death is but one facet of eternal life. It is believed that all living beings, animals included, undergo a continuing cycle of birth and death. For Buddhists, therefore, death is thought to be not so much the end of an existence as the beginning of a new one. Bhuddhism believes that every living entity, plants included, contain the seeds of Buddhahood, the highest life condition.

RITUALS AND CEREMONIES

Thoughout history all cultures have consecrated human death with a ceremony or ritual of some kind. Many people feel it appropriate to do the same for a loved pet. The RSPCA was founded by the Reverend Arthur Broome, an Anglican priest and the society's first secretary. He was motivated entirely by the Christian faith and Christian principles. For those who would find it helpful, the RSPCA produces a booklet entitled *Order of Service for Animal Welfare*, written and compiled by the Revd Professor Andrew Linzey. It is suitable for most Christian denominations and includes prayers and bible passages appropriate to a burial service. I particularly liked this quote of St Bonaventura (1221-1274): 'Every creature is by its nature a kind of effigy and likeness of the eternal Wisdom.'

The Egyptians buried cats with the same ceremony accorded to human beings. In her book *The Cult of the Cat*, Patricia Dale-Green describes, in detail, the embalming procedure. After being treated with drugs and spices, a rich man's cat was wrapped in an elaborate shroud with a papier-mache mask covering the head, then placed in a painted mummy case. A poor man's cat made do with a simple sheet of plain linen. It was also customary for those in whose house a cat had died to shave their eyebrows. This was done partly as an outward sign of mourning, but also as a form of superstitious magic. The soft hair of the eyebrows both resembled the fur of the departed creature and had the same crescent form as the ancient symbol of the moon.

The most famous of the cat cemeteries, visited by the Greek historian Herodotus in 450 BC, was at Bubatis, in the Nile delta. Another vast cemetery containing over 50,000 mummified cats was discovered in Tel Benii-Hassan during the last century. Tragically, this ancient burial ground was ransacked and the bodies destroyed. It was an act of mindless barbarism that resulted in a great loss to archaeology and deprived the world of an irreplaceable treasure.

The Buddhist ceremony for the death of any living creature is based on the fundamental principle that life is eternal. It involves chanting to change the pet's karma, as well as prayers that it should be reborn in the best possible circumstances.

There are those, of course, who do not wish to bury their pet with a religious or overtly spiritual ceremony. In this case, simply remembering their animal with love – and perhaps planting a memorial tree or shrub in a favourite part of the garden – allows them to dignify the occasion and release some of the emotion they feel.

Ultimately, death and bereavement are inevitabilities we all have to accept. Painful though they are, they can also teach us to treasure life and not take it for granted. Each cat is an individual, and some of us will share our homes with several during the course of our lives. Another animal cannot replace the creature we have lost, nor should we want it to. To welcome a new cat means opening our lives to a new relationship. It means accepting that where there is an end, there can also be a new beginning.

Chapter 8

THE PROBLEM OF CAT LOVERS WHO LOVE TOO MUCH

SUBSTITUTE BABIES AND IDEALISED LOVE OBJECTS

As George Bernard Shaw observed, animals 'bear more than their natural burden of human love'. This is particularly true of the animals we share our homes with, those small, affectionate, cuddle-sized, strokable creatures we refer to collectively as 'pets'. Loving Puss or Felix is not a problem – indeed, the giving and receiving of love is an integral part of the feline/human relationship. But it's when that love becomes disproportionate, when the cat loses its animal identity to become a child substitute or an object of adoration, that the situation is no longer emotionally healthy.

Our society has undergone enormous changes over the last few decades. The break-up of the nuclear

97

family, the falling birth rate and the disintegration of traditional communities have resulted in a situation where large sections of the population live alone. As a consequence, we have more people suffering from stress, loneliness and feelings of alienation than ever before. Research shows that it is the childless, the 'empty-nesters' and the isolated elderly that are most likely to become emotionally dependent on their pets. The animal becomes the focus of their whole world, a substitute for the nurturing outlet or human contact they are lacking. In these circumstances the animal risks being smothered, over-indulged and generally lavished with all the emotion that that particular human heart needs to express.

Mrs Miles, an elderly woman of my acquaintance, is such an example. After many adventurous years working abroad (she is fluent in French and German), she returned to England in her mid-30s, married a schoolteacher and started a family. When she was 65 her husband died and a year later her daughter fell in love with an Australian and went to live in Perth. Her son, with whom she doesn't get on, visits only at Christmas and birthdays. The neighbours with whom she was friendly have either died or moved away. With the exception of the old gentleman who still lives in the house opposite, she knows no one in her street any more.

We met when her husband was still alive and she was doing the odd translation to supplement his pension. B.B. (called after Brigitte Bardot whom Mrs Miles met several times in her capacity as personal secretary to a wealthy Parisian socialite) was a four-month-old kitten

and, like all kittens, extremely lively. Mrs Miles adored her, of course, but would stand for no nonsense. In fact, I remember her being banished from the room after her third attempt to jump on the table while we were having tea.

Seven years later the situation is very different. B.B. is now treated as a sort of invalid child whose particular requirements only Mrs Miles understands. Each and every day is dedicated to B.B.'s presumed needs. Her basket, piled high with satin cushions, hogs the fire, while a similarly bedecked doll's pram is frequently used to wheel her around the house. B.B. is constantly checked on, petted (often to her irritation), and all communication is in baby talk. The last time I visited, Mrs Miles was preparing herself a supper of baked beans on toast. B.B., on the other hand, had just finished tucking in to poached salmon steak and a saucer of double cream. I was told that the reason for this 'little treat' was that B.B. had been 'rather depressed'. Mrs Miles has very little money. She deprives herself of essentials to give B.B. only the best.

The ascribing of human needs and emotions to animals has a name: anthropomorphism. It is an inappropriate displacement of feelings and affection that distorts the correct animal/human relationship and causes problems for them, too. For animals the main negative is probably overfeeding. In his book *Pets and Their People*, veterinary surgeon Bruce Fogel talks about cats and dogs so stuffed with rich diets that they are unable to cope with ailments which otherwise would not have been fatal. They were, he says bluntly, 'killed by kindness'.

CAT COLLECTORS

Another distortion is cat collecting. This does not mean having three, four or even five cats. It means turning your home into a colony for literally dozens of unspayed, uncastrated and uncontrolled animals. Cat Collectors are usually people who have decided that the human race is universally rotten and that animals possess all the virtues. They go on to create an alternative feline society of which they can feel comfortably a part. This happened to a childhood friend who descended into misanthropic alcoholism when, after 11 years, her lover left her for another woman. Within a month of moving back with her widowed mother she had filled the house with 27 strays.

Four years later, aged 33, she suffered a mental breakdown and spent a period in a psychiatric hospital. When she came out she was able to resume her career and – with two cats only – lead a more or less normal life. Her mother had meanwhile enlisted the help of The Cats Protection League to resolve the desperate cat colony problem.

This sort of Cat Collector is almost always eccentric. Very often they distrust vets and will not take their sick animals for treatment. And, like Mrs Miles, they consistently neglect their own most basic needs in the service of their animals. When my friend was taken to hospital her mental state was such that she hardly knew what was going on and, therefore, couldn't object. Cat Collectors who fall physically ill, however, frequently refuse to go into hospital for fear of what will happen to their animals in their absence.

The 18th-century English philosopher Jeremy Bentham was not a Cat Collector. He was, however, a misanthropist who had little respect for his fellow humans, considering most of them a waste of time. The only creature he really valued was his cat, Langbourne. This esteem was reflected in the way he addressed him. The philosopher first called his animal 'Sir John Langbourne', later elevating his status to 'The Reverend Sir John Langbourne'. He would certainly have approved the sentiments in the following poem.

I think I could turn and live with animals, they are so placid and self-contain'd

102

I stand and look at them long and long
They do not sweat and whine about their condition,
They do not lie awake in the dark and weep for their sins,
They do not make me sick discussing their duty to God,
Not one is dissatisfied, not one is demented with the mania of owning things,
Not one kneels to another, nor to his kind that lived thousands of years ago,
Not one is respectable or unhappy over the whole earth.

Song of Myself, 32

TUG OF WAR LOVE

In 1987, Janet Harris split up with her live-in lover. They had no problem dividing up the china, linen or record collection, but could not agree on who should take Chocolate Drop, the cat. She was eventually 'catnapped' by Ken Walker, who refused to give her back. The question was finally taken to the Bournemouth County Court. Mr Walker contested that, given that he had found the cat wandering as a stray in 1985, she was rightfully his. Ms Harris retorted that as she had registered her with the Burmese Cat Club in her name, Chocolate Drop belonged to her. The judge ruled in Ms Harris's favour and ordered that Chocolate Drop be returned home.

In this situation, Chocolate Drop was the surrogate child and both 'parents' had made an emotional investment in her. Like many divorcing couples fighting over custody of kids, consideration of Chocolate Drop didn't really come into it. She was the prize possession and neither wanted the other to have her.

Friends of mine faced a similar situation when they split up. They also 'parented' their cat – who just so happened to be a Burmese, too. In their case, however, they were eventually able to come up with an amicable solution. Smokey, it was decided, would spend alternate weeks in Clapham with Lynn and in Forest Hill with Adrian. Two years on, this arrangement is still up and running and Smokey gives no sign that he objects. At Lynn's, he enjoys the company of a pair of sluggish terrapins and the permission to snooze on her desk

while she works. At Adrian's, he has a garden with a tree to climb and a fascinating tool shed to explore. Indeed, Smokey has become so used to the to-ing and fro-ing that he's long stopped using his cat basket. Instead he sits, keen and alert, on the back seat of Adrian's car, making appreciative little noises as he stares out of the window.

A sadder problem in relationships is the pet who becomes the butt of frustration and displaced anger. In these situations the disfunctional owner responds to problems with his or her partner by kicking or shouting at the cat. Sometimes one party nurtures extreme dislike for the creature simply because the other loves it.

CAT PROBLEMS

The Green-eyed Monster

Cats are renowned for their beauty, grace, dignity and aloofness. They are also renowned for their jealousy. Anyone who has shared living space with a cat knows how jealous it can become of its people and its territory. Forced to share either of these with someone or something else, it is a safe bet it will react badly. A profound and prolonged sulk is one way that it communicates the strength of its wounded feelings. Another is the venting of spleen in anti-social behaviour. This can take the form of territory spraying, fouling the house and even aggression. It is in everybody's interests, therefore, to be particularly considerate of Puss's feelings when new members are added to a family.

Pete and his burly tabby tom, Willie, had lived a comfortable, if domestically chaotic, life together before Hilary moved in. There were just the two of them and Willie forgave Pete those odd occasions when, for one reason or another, he wasn't fed. Most nights Willie was out prowling, except if it was raining, and then he slept curled at the bottom of Pete's bed. Although neither was overly demonstrative to the other, Willie spent many a half-hour sprawled across Pete's chest sucking the sleeve of his woollen jumper.

While Hilary was just a visitor, Willie was prepared to tolerate her. When she took up residence, however, he was enormously put out. The fact that her presence had benefits for him – she not only fed him regularly, she upgraded his whole diet – was beside the point. At first all he did was stalk around bristling with indignation and hostility. On the occasions they found themselves in the living room together, he would sit a few feet away with his back turned firmly against her. Then one day, without warning and just when she thought she was winning him over, he sprang at her, sinking his teeth and claws in her leg.

Willie's aggression was totally unpredictable, often manifesting after Hilary had given him his carefully prepared food. Her legs were soon covered with nasty scars and she became quite fearful of him, so much so that Pete thought he had no alternative but to find

Willie another home. After two or three months, however, things began to settle down. Nowadays, although he still makes the occasional hissing lunge, Hilary and Willie manage to cohabit in reasonable harmony.

If cats get jealous of an adult interloper, it is nothing to what they can feel when a cat-sized human creature suddenly appears to monopolise everyone's attention. This is potentially more serious and must be handled sensitively from the start. Firstly – to make sure Puss doesn't feel miffed or pushed out – find a little time to give her some fuss and affection. Then satisfy her curiosity by introducing her carefully to the new baby.

Although it's extremely rare for a cat to attack a baby, it has happened, so don't leave them alone together. In fact, even if your cat feels no animosity, it's a good idea to put some cat-proof netting over the cot and pram. Sometimes a cat will lie on top of a baby because it is attracted by its warmth. Inadvertent suffocation is the commonest tragedy involving cats and babies.

Inappropriate Elimination
'Inappropriate Elimination' is the term used by animal behaviourists to describe urinating on the carpet or defecating on Gran's treasured needlepoint cushion. Before anything else it is important to rule out a physical cause. These can be inflammation of the bladder or urethra, blocked anal sacs, illness, physical injury, and hormonal changes. Once these have been

excluded, then it is likely your cat is protesting about
something disruptive in its environment. Jealousy, as we
have seen, is one cause for this sort of unwelcome
behaviour. Other reasons range from the brand of litter
being changed, to stray cats hanging around the
vicinity, or simply a strong objection to the living-room
furniture being rearranged.

It can also be a communication of hostility. When
Micia was a kitten my husband took a job in the north
of Italy which meant he was only home at weekends. No
great animal lover, he was indifferent to cats – except if
they tried to sit or lie on him and then he couldn't
stand them. Micia, for her part, expressed her opinion

of him by plonking herself on his chest the moment he fell asleep and defecating under his chair in the dining room.

Micia's 'inappropriate elimination' occurred every Friday in anticipation of my husband's arrival. On all other days she was perfectly well behaved. I was amazed by her ability to keep track of the week and the fact she always managed to do her dirty deed without being caught in the act. It was clear that the furore the subsequent discovery of her deposit provoked gratified her, for she usually appeared the moment she heard his outraged and disgusted voice. After a few minutes of lazily observing the frantic clean-up operation, she would then turn her head and stare with feigned indifference out of the window. My response to this display was always a mixture of fury and admiration. I would look at that haughty profile and find myself thinking: Now that's style!

notquite so lucky black cat

Chapter 9

DID YOU KNOW THAT ... ?

SUPERSTITION

In Britain and Europe black cats are considered lucky, in America white ones are. In the East it is tortoiseshell cats that are the portents of good fortune.

In the south of France people believed that anyone who gave food and shelter to a matagot (a magician's cat) would receive great prosperity in return.

Japanese sailors always tried to take a tortoiseshell cat on voyages with them. Not only did they expect it would give them forewarning of any imminent storms, they believed it was actually capable of frightening the fierce storm demons away.

English sailors believed that if the ship's cat licked its

fur in the wrong direction or scratched the table legs with its claws this would start a furious storm. If a cat on board ship was actually thrown overboard the result would be a tempest.

The first English trial for witchcraft took place in 1566 during the the reign of Elizabeth I. Agnes Waterhouse and her daughter Joan were found guilty of being linked in witchcraft with a 'whyte spotted catte' which they fed with 'breade and milke ... and call it by the name of Sathan'. They were both executed.

In 1607 Edward Topsell advised the following to cure a disease of the eye: 'Take the head of a blacke Cat, which hath not a spot of another colour in it, and burne it to a powder in an earthen pot leaded or glazed within, then take this powder and through a quill blow it thrice a day into they eie ... and so shall all paine fly away.'

According to superstitious folklore, if the tail of a black cat is buried under the front doorstep, it will protect the house and its occupants from illness. It is also said that the skin of a black cat, applied directly to rheumaticky joints, will relieve the pain. Another old wives' tale says the blood of a black cat will cure hives.

Venetia Newell, in her book on animal folklore, records that the wives of some Scarborough sailors kept black cats to ensure their husband's safety at sea.

According to an ancient Cornish custom a person who encounters an unfamiliar black cat should draw a cross on the toe of their shoe as a protection against ill fortune.

It is said that when a cat deserts a house, it is because it knows one of the occupants is about to die.

The witch-hunters of the Middle Ages believed cats were agents of the Devil. The night shine of their eyes, they said, was nothing less than a reflection of the fires of hell. In his *Histoire of Foure-footed Beasts* (1607), Edward Topsell said that their '... eies glitter above measure ... when a man commeth to see a cat on the sudden, and in the night; they can hardly be endured, for their flaming aspect'.

Edward Topsell also told his readers that if, while grooming, a cat should 'put her feete beyond the crowne of her head, it is a presage of rain'.

The Indonesians believed cats were capable of inducing rain. They held special rituals in which cats were carried three times in procession around a parched field, after which they were dunked in water to remind them of their connection with that element.

For Eastern Europeans, lightning bolts were the work of angels trying to exorcise the evil spirits which took possession of cats during thunderstorms. For this reason cats were quickly hustled outside when a storm broke. If the angels were targeting the cat, people reasoned, it was far safer for them and their possessions if the animal was out of the house.

An old English country superstition said that cats could sour milk and bring down plagues of insects to destroy the crops.

Some modern-day occultists believe that all cats are psychic and have access to a spiritual realm which ordinary people are denied. This is how they are able to pick up on dangers which, although manifesting on a 'psychic plane', haven't yet materialised on the physical plane. They maintain that it is this sensibility which allows a cat to alert its owner to impending dangers such as earthquakes and air-raids.

An old British saying is, 'Whenever the cat of the house is black, the lasses of lovers will have no lack.'

RELIGION

In 1988 a tabby walked into a Buddhist temple in Kuala Lumpur, Malaysia, and joined the monks gathered in meditation. In a feline approximation of the lotus position – squatting on its haunches, front paws pressed together – it has joined every midday meditation session since. The monks believe the cat is the reincarnation of an ancient Buddha.

Freyja, the Scandinavian goddess of love and beauty, daughter of Niord and Skadi and sister of Frey, the male fertility god, rode in a chariot drawn by a team of magnificent cats. To ensure good crops and favourable weather, farmers would leave out offerings for the animals.

The congregation of a Lincolnshire church were surprised and amused when a small Tortie Burmese began turning up every Sunday and taking her place on the back pew. She would sit erect and attentive all through the long service, slipping out quietly with everyone else at the end. The cat became such a talking point that eventually the new vicar had to confess that the feline worshipper belonged to him.

At first Honey had seemed like a normal kitten: curious, vocal and adventurous like all her breed. But

soon she was manifesting what could only be described as a religious vocation. She became enraptured when the vicar played choir music, listened intently when he rehearsed his sermons, and always insisted on following him to church. The parishioners loved Honey but the presence of a pious cat in the House of God made the clergyman's superiors distinctly uneasy. All attempts to keep her at home failed, however, and she became a regular and respected member of the congregation.

Once upon a time every temple in Japan kept a cat to guard its holy manuscripts from the attentions of hungry mice. Maneki-Neko was one such temple cat who became famous throughout the land for the skill with which she waylaid passers-by and lured them to her lowly temple. Many visitors meant many donations and Maneki-Neko's temple soon became rich. In honour of Maneki-Neko's memory, the temple was turned into a cat cemetery and shrine, a Mecca for Tokyo cat-lovers who bring offerings and small cat figures to help their departed pets on their way to heaven. Painted on the temple facade are row upon row of cats. All are portrayed with raised paws to represent Maneki-Neko's gesture of greeting, now also a symbol of good luck.

The ancient Peruvian god of fertility and healing, Ai Apaec, was a combination of old man and tom cat.

There is a Buddhist tradition which says that the house which has a light-coloured cat will always have silver and that a dark-coloured cat will ensure the house never lacks gold.

The only animal allowed to the female hermits under the strict discipline of the Cistercian order was the cat. 'Ye mine leove sustren,' says the Ancren Riwle (Anchoress's Rule), 'ne schulen haben no Best bute Kat one.' (You my beloved sisters, shall have no beast but one cat.)

There is a popular legend which says that while Mary gave birth to Jesus in the stable, a mother cat was giving birth to a kitten. There are many charming paintings inspired by this legend showing the Jesus Child playing with a kitten. Of these the most famous is the beautiful *The Madonna of the Cat*. It is the work of the 16th-century Urbanese painter, Federico Baroccio, and now hangs in London's National Gallery. It depicts the young St John teasing a cat with a captive bird to amuse the child Jesus.

Some Siamese cats have small marks on their fur at a point just below the back of the neck. Cats with these marks are considered particularly sacred by Siamese priests. They call the marks 'Temple Marks', saying the first ones were made when the cat was picked up by a deity.

Although Mafdet was the first Egyptian cat deity, Bast (also called Basht, Bastet or Pascht) is the most famous. Depicted as having the head of a cat and the body of a woman, Bast signified the fruitful powers of the sun. To devotees of her cult, all cats were considered sacred and treated as such. Her temples teemed with them and there were special priestesses whose job it was to take care of their welfare. The annual spring festival held at Bubastis was attended by 700,000 of the goddess's worshippers. It was also believed that on certain occasions the cat was entrusted to lead the souls of the dead to Paradise.

There is a story which says Mohammed was so fond of his cat that when it fell asleep on the sleeve of his robe, he cut off the sleeve in preference to disturbing the cat.

HISTORICAL

Ancient Egyptians hunting in the marshes of the delta trained cats to act as retrievers. One of the wall paintings from Nebamen's tomb at Thebes (c 1400 BC) depicts the hunting cats that his subjects are confident he will find waiting for him in his afterlife.

In time of war, the animal kingdom's highest decoration is the Dicken Medal awarded by the PDSA for gallantry in the face of the enemy. During the Second World War it was awarded to 18 dogs, 31 pigeons and one ship's cat.

One thousand years ago, King Henry I of Saxony decreed that anyone who killed an adult cat should be fined the hefty sum of 60 bushels of corn.

The Welsh king, Hywel Dda, wrote his famous *Laws* around AD 700 and they were translated into modern English in the 19th century. This is what they say about the cat: 'The price of a cat is four pence. Her qualities are to see, to hear, to kill mice, to have her claws whole, and to nurse and not devour her kittens. If she be deficient in any one of these qualities, one third of her price must be returned.'

The first cat show was held at the Crystal Palace in London in 1871 and became an annual event. The first British Cat Club was founded in 1887. The British Council for the Cat Fancy was formed from the National Cat Club in 1910 and lays down the rules governing all breeds.

Japan's first cats were imported from China in the 10th century. For several centuries only the nobility were allowed to own them, with the result that they were outrageously pampered and indulged. According to Lafcadio Hearn, the common name for a pet cat was *tama*, which means jewel.

In 17th-century Turkey, cats were treated with the greatest of consideration and respect. Leading citizens got together to establish institutions dedicated to providing the feline population with care and support. They even established special houses for those free-spirited cats who wished to roam as they pleased during the day but wanted a little comfort and shelter at night.

At the end of the last century an estimated 300,000 mummified cats were found at Beni Hassan and many thousands more were excavated at Bubastis. They were sold at the price of $18.43 per ton and sent by the boatload to England. Because of the glut they were little appreciated. After distribution to museums large and small, the rest were ground up for fertiliser or used as ballast for ships. Out of one consignment of 19 tons of mummified cats imported to England, only one skull survives. This is now in the Natural History Museum.

In 1344 an outbreak of St Vitus's Dance in the French town of Metz caused the citizens to spend their days twitching and prancing. When the epidemic was at its peak a knight rode into town and took lodgings in one of the inns. That evening, just as he was about to fall asleep, an enormous black cat suddenly appeared on the nearby hearth and stared fixedly at him. Leaping to his feet, the knight made the sign of the cross and drew his sword. The cat, hissing foul blasphemies, immediately disappeared. The following day the knight left the inn to discover that the epidemic was over. This convinced him that the cat had been the devil in disguise and by banishing him he had freed the town of its curse. The city authorities agreed and proceeded to round up cats for a public burning. Every year for more than 400 years afterwards the people of Metz celebrated that day by imprisoning 13 cats in an iron cage and burning them on a great bonfire built on the esplanade.

English Protestants who were taking part in the 1559 coronation of Elizabeth I, brought with them a wicker effigy of the Pope which they carried in procession and finally burned on a pyre. The effigy was inside a wicker cage with live cats who 'squalled in a most hideous manner as soon as they felt the fire'. These cries were described as 'the language of the devils within the body of the Holy Father'.

Alexander the Great, Napoleon and Hitler were all rabid cat-haters.

TOPICAL

According to R C Hatch of the University of Guelph in Ontario, a constituent of catnip is a volatile oil called trans cis nepetalactone, which has a molecular structure similar to that of LSD. He suggests that cats who begin behaving bizarrely after ingesting some – like chasing around in circles or trying to catch phantom butterflies – may simply be experiencing the feline equivalent of a hallucinogenic trip.

In 1987 the Cats Protection League (CLP) found homes
for over 47,000 cats (feral and domesticated) and had
just over 27,000 neutered. The league said that the
number of cats in Britain who have gone feral after
being abandoned is growing. There are literally
thousands of colonies of them now in London. Hospital
grounds and factory sites are the favourite breeding
grounds.

More than 10,000 cats are employed by the British
Government to keep official buildings free from rodents.

In 1980 it was revealed that the CIA had trained cats to carry bombs. This information was contained in documents released to the American public under the Freedom of Information Act.

In 1989 organised cat thieves supplying the cat fur market, vivisectionists, and people involved in illegal dog fights (the cats are used as bait) targeted Eastbourne, Worthing, Bridlington and Wrexham. Two years earlier, over a four-week period more than 100 cats went missing in Lewisham and Greenwich in South London. Particularly at risk are tortoiseshell, tabby and white cats.

When, in 1986, Morris the Cat was drafted as a Democratic candidate for the presidency of the United States of America, polls showed he had the highest name recognition and approval rating among the American public of any of the candidates so far declared. Announcing Morris's decision to seek the nomination, the feline's communications director said: 'The world is going to the dogs. America needs a President with courage who won't pussyfoot around the issues of peace – a president who, when adversity arises, will always land on his feet.'

Ms Eleanor Mondale, daughter of former Vice-President Mondale, made a statement on Morris's behalf. 'Morris realises prejudices exist but he believes, like records, they are meant to be broken. Morris gives the examples of Harry S Truman who, in 1948, became the first haberdasher to inhabit the Oval Office, and John Kennedy who became the first Catholic president in 1962.' Despite his great popularity, however, Morris didn't manage to make it to the White House.

PHYSIOLOGY

Edward Topsell writes admiringly of how the cat 'whurleth with her voyce, having as many tunes as turnes, for she hath one voice to beg and complain, another to testifie her delight and pleasure, another among her own kind ... insomuch as some have thought that [cats] have a particular intelligible language among themselves.'

There are two theories as to how a cat purrs, but science still doesn't know for sure. One theory says purring is produced by the membrane folds – the so-called false vocal cord – that lie behind the ordinary vocal cords in the cat's larynx. It is the inhaled and exhaled air passing over these membrane folds that gives rise to that wonderful soft rumbling we all so adore.

The second theory is slightly more bizarre. It maintains that the larynx has nothing to do with it: purring is caused by turbulent blood. This blood turbulence is supposed to occur when an increased blood-flow is constricted by the main vein as it passes through the cat's chest. The diaphragm acts as an amplifier to the swirling blood, echoing the sound up through windpipe and sinus cavities and producing the purr.

The cat's optical system is extremely sensitive and considerably more efficient than our own. Their angle of view for each eye is over 200 degrees. As hunting animals, their eyesight is especially sensitive to night vision. In the dark their pupil appears as a very wide aperture, in bright sunlight it is a narrow, vertical slit. A

cat is able to gather light in what looks to us like
absolute darkness.
Cats' eyes shine in the dark because of a reflective layer
at the back of the retina called the tapetum lucidum,
which acts like a mirror.

In the prime of life a human ear can discern noises up
to about 20,000 cycles per second. Cats, on the other
hand, can hear sounds up to 100,000 cycles per second.
Young cats also have the ability to pinpoint the precise
direction of a noise with extraordinary accuracy. They
can distinguish between two sounds which are only 18
inches apart at a distance of 60 feet; they can separate
two sounds coming from the same direction but at
different distances; and they can differentiate two
sounds that have only a half-tone difference between
them.

The rate of a cat's heartbeat is 110 to 130 times per
minute, one third again as fast as the human heart.

In his book *Catlore* Desmond Morris says the reason
white cats are reputed to make bad mothers is because a
large proportion of them are deaf. Therefore, it is not
that they are callously ignoring their offspring's cries
for attention, they simply do not hear them.
Tortoiseshell cats are almost always female. The ratio of
males to females has been calculated at 200-1. When a
male tortoiseshell does occur, it is almost always sterile.
This is due to an extra X chromosome which gives the

animal a genetic constitution of XXY. The Y chromosome endows the cat with maleness, but the double Xs make it sterile.

The ideal temperature for feline food is 86 degrees F, the same temperature as the cat's tongue.

Bibliography

ADAMOLI, Vida
Amazing Animals (Robson Books, London 1989)

BEADLE ,Muriel
The Cat (Simon & Schuster Inc, New York 1977)

THE CATS PROTECTION LEAGUE
A Passion for Cats (David & Charles, London 1987)

DAY, Christopher
Natural Remedies for Your Cat (Piccadilly Press Ltd, London 1994)

FOGEL, Bruce
Pets and Their People (Collins Harvill, London 1983)

GETTING, Fred
The Secret Lore of the Cat (Grafton Books, London 1989)

LOXTON, Howard
The Beauty of Cats (Tribune Press, London 1972)

MORRIS, Desmond
Catlore (Jonathan Cape, London 1987)

STEVENS, John Richard
The Enchanted Cat (Prima Publishing and
Communications, CA 1990)

WOLFF, HG, DVM
Your Healthy Cat, Homeopathic Medicines for Common
Feline Ailments (North Atlantic Books, CA 1991)

Other cat books published by Piccadilly Press

NATURAL REMEDIES FOR YOUR CAT
by Christopher Day MA VetMB, MRCVS, VetFFHom
Illustrated by Anuk Naumann

Can you help your cat recover from food poisoning?
What can you do when your cat has an abscess?
How can you combat fleas?

For anyone wanting to use more nautral remedies and
home help for their cat, this elegant, beautifully-
illustrated book is a must.

As well as giving advice on the treatment of many
ailments, Christopher Day, a qualified veterinary
surgeon, explains the remedies – Homoeopathic,
Essential Oils, Herbal, Bach Flower and Biochemic Tissue
Salts – and discusses diet and life style.

If you have problems finding this book, send a cheque
for £8.99 to Piccadilly Press Ltd., (£7.99 plus £1.00 for
p&p).